What people are saying about …

ADDICTED TO BUSY

"Like everyone who is running hard and fast after Jesus, I am reminded by Pastor Brady that rhythmic patterns of life are essential to do the strenuous work of the gospel. May we fight for a Sabbath rest in our lives so that we will be reinvigorated to continue to push forward in our destiny and purpose."

Christine Caine, founder of The A21 Campaign
and bestselling author of *Undaunted*

"I know what this addiction is all about, and I know the cost I have paid for it too. These words will help you get free from one of the most 'sanctified' bondages in the church. The relief alone is worth it."

John Eldredge, bestselling
author of *Wild at Heart*

"*Addicted to Busy* is packed with biblical insights and practical steps to help you establish a rhythmic life. Read it and embrace the joy that comes from staying in tune with your Creator."

John and Lisa Bevere, Messenger International

BRADY BOYD

ADDICTED TO BUSY

Recovery for the Rushed Soul

David C Cook
transforming lives together

ADDICTED TO BUSY
Published by David C Cook
4050 Lee Vance View
Colorado Springs, CO 80918 U.S.A.

David C Cook Distribution Canada
55 Woodslee Avenue, Paris, Ontario, Canada N3L 3E5

David C Cook U.K., Kingsway Communications
Eastbourne, East Sussex BN23 6NT, England

The graphic circle C logo is a registered trademark of David C Cook.

The website addresses recommended throughout this book are offered as a
resource to you. These websites are not intended in any way to be or imply an
endorsement on the part of David C Cook, nor do we vouch for their content.

Unless otherwise noted, all Scripture quotations are taken from *THE MESSAGE*.
Copyright © by Eugene H. Peterson 1993, 2002. Used by permission of NavPress
Publishing Group. Scripture quotations marked NIV are taken from the Holy Bible,
New International Version®, NIV®. Copyright © 1973, 2011 by Biblica, Inc.™ Used
by permission of Zondervan. All rights reserved worldwide. www.zondervan.com.

LCCN 2014940401
ISBN 978-0-7814-1034-2
eISBN 978-0-7814-1167-7

The Author is represented by the literary agency of Alive
Communications, Inc., 7680 Goddard Street, Suite 200, Colorado
Springs, CO 80920. www.alivecommunications.com.

The Team: Alex Field, John Blase, Helen Macdonald, Amy Konyndyk, Karen Athen
Cover Design: Nick Lee

Printed in the United States of America
First Edition 2014

2 3 4 5 6 7 8 9 10

020515

For Pam, my bride and best friend

CONTENTS

Take it easy.
Don't let the sound of your own wheels
drive you crazy.
Lighten up while you still can.

—The Eagles

ACKNOWLEDGMENTS

I am very grateful for the team at David C Cook who believed in this book and took a chance on me. Thank you for speaking life into this manuscript.

Thank you, Ashley Wiersma, for helping me skillfully craft these chapters. Your expertise and wisdom have been invaluable, as always, and I appreciate your passion for this message of rest, Sabbath, and sustainability. Your labor of love for this book is revealed on every page.

To my tribe at New Life Church, thanks for allowing me to live with healthy rhythms as I serve as your pastor. Your gift to me of a sabbatical was truly life-giving and will empower me to function faithfully alongside you with renewed vitality and vision.

Thank you, Abram and Callie. You are gifts from the Lord to your mom and me, and I find rest and strength each time I am with you. I love you both, forever and always.

INTRODUCTION

This Book Won't Change Your Life

I'm a complete hypocrite for writing this book because I don't actually live out the restful rhythms I so passionately espouse. However, I *do* recognize that digging in my heels and demanding self-discipline will never correct my errant ways. These behaviors can't and won't correct your errant ways either, which is why I can so boldly declare that this book will not change your life. Books don't change our lives.

Here's what will change our rhythms, our pace, our lives: revelation from the Spirit of God, or, in other words, the ability to detect spiritually what we've had only sensory knowledge of before. Yes, life is made up of tasks on the to-do list, kids rattling off their incessant needs and wants, the hurried embrace of a spouse who is rushing off to carpool, the scent of one more bag of fast food—really, now, who has time to cook anymore?

But life also involves an undercurrent, a spiritual underpinning holding together our days. It's the "God story" that contextualizes the

"Us story." It's a spiritual understanding that makes our lives make sense. The highest goal I can set for this book is that it will somehow serve as a conduit for the revelation we so sorely need. Mere words on a page can't talk us out of our beloved freneticism, but the Holy Spirit can, and *will*, if we let him.

I want this revelation, and yet I don't, because on the heels of real revelation, real-deal growth is required. "Revelation is not for the faint at heart," wrote Anne Lamott. But how beautiful it is when it finally appears. Without it, Anne said, "life can seem like an endless desert of danger with scratchy sand in your shoes, and yet if we remember or are reminded to pay attention, we find so many sources of hidden water, so many bits and chips and washes of color, in a weed or the gravel or a sunrise. There are so many ways to sweep the sand off our feet. So we say, 'Oh my God. Thanks.'"[1]

That sense of gratitude is what I desperately want to feel. I want to receive revelation, I want to live from revelation, and I want to thank God for gently prodding me to slow my pace, saving my sanity. And yet here are a couple of questions I mull over: *Would I even know how to live a slowed-down life? Would I know what to do with rest?* When I was first handed my newborn son, even though I was instantly in love with him, there was this question rushing through my brain: *What does it do?*

Would I look at a well-rested life the same way?

How do I hold it?

What is it good for?

What on earth does it do?

I wonder if I'd be the guy who would unravel with the quiet of it all.

Still, I'm willing to try. I'm willing to put on a rhythmic life. As Maya Angelou said, in her unfailingly poetic way, "When you know better, you do better." I've known better for a long, long time; I'm ready for the doing-better part to begin.

In Jewish tradition, the command to "keep the Sabbath holy" is followed religiously, beginning at sundown Friday and lasting a full twenty-four hours, until sundown Saturday. Friday evening, as a way to welcome the prescribed unplug, the family recites a blessing—kiddush, it's called, literally meaning "holy." There's a kiddush cup that you use, which looks like an ornate goblet that's been glued to a small saucer—a saucer that's really important, not only in function but also in form. When the blessing is recited, typically the father of the family pours wine into the goblet until it overflows, spilling out. You can get the cup and saucer for fifteen bucks on Amazon, but you can get what it represents only by living a rhythmic life. The pouring out, the overflow, the blessing—the symbol here as the Sabbath begins is that God's abundance cannot be contained.

This is what I'm after: Feeling not empty, but full. Living not at full throttle, but at rest. Letting whatever abundance God has in store for me come in, sit down, and be at home.

PART ONE: DISEASE
Burnout as a Status Symbol

We are so busy.
Usually too busy for God.

—Leonard Sweet

1

DEAD HUSBAND WALKING

There is more to life than increasing its speed.
—Mahatma Gandhi

FIGHTING HEALTHY RHYTHMS

I began fighting what I call "rhythmic living"—living intentionally, sanely, and at peace—at an early age. The childhood version of me was a boy who was always moving, always doing, and always lacking appreciation for rest. There was a horse to ride through the woods, and there were deer to hunt and fish to catch. What use was slowing down and reflecting on things, when all this life was waiting to be lived?

As I morphed into a teenager, my pace only intensified. I was born with a heart condition and found I had to work twice as hard as my buddies in order to achieve the same sports-related goals. So I pushed, pushed, pushed, insisting my body run faster, go farther, and play harder. Intellectually, I was exactly the same way. I pushed just as hard in both high school and college, always hungering and thirsting for more information, more knowledge, more understanding of this thing called life. I wasn't naturally smart, but I was naturally curious. Curiosity dictated my pace in life, and curiosity never sits down.

My wife, Pam, and I married when we were twenty-two, and within five years, I was running my life at unprecedented speeds, even for me. We lived in Shreveport, Louisiana, at the time, where I taught junior- and senior-level English literature at Evangel Christian Academy, a prep school with several hundred children. That role alone would have meant a full plate for me, but I treated it as a mere side dish, adding to it half a dozen other appetizing things. I was the boys' varsity basketball coach. I was the girls' varsity basketball coach. I was the boys' JV basketball coach and also the junior high boys' basketball coach. I was the high school track-and-field coach, one of the campus pastors for the school, and the volunteer youth pastor at the church associated with the school.

These combined commitments meant I was gone from six or seven in the morning until ten or eleven at night, teaching, conducting parent-teacher conferences, grading papers, tutoring students, leading practices, driving buses, coaching games, washing uniforms in the locker room's laundry facility, and more. During that season of life, the greatest compliment you could have paid me was, "Wow. You're always so busy." To me, busyness equaled movement, and movement was necessary for me to get ahead.

I had exactly one day off a week, which was Saturday. But even then, I refused to rest.

The pastor of the church where I served as volunteer youth pastor was a man twenty years my senior, a man I idolized to such an extent it bordered on unhealthy. I wanted to be this guy. He was (and remains) the best preacher I've ever heard and was an all-around amazing man. One weekend he approached me and invited me to have breakfast with him the following morning. I was blown away that he would even talk to me, let alone want to spend time one-on-one. I said yes immediately.

In the early 1990s, the governor of Louisiana, Buddy Roemer, had declared solving the crime problem in New Orleans and Shreveport as one of his primary initiatives. These cities were, at the time, among the top crime centers in the entire country. These were dark, dark places, and Governor Roemer was determined to shine some light.

He enlisted the aid of local church pastors to head up a volunteer crime-fighting force in the state's most dangerous, most vulnerable communities, and my pastor happened to be one of the pastors involved. When I met him for breakfast at the diner on Kings Highway, he said, "Brady, Governor Roemer would like our church to participate in fighting crime, and one of the ways I'd like to do that is by starting an adopt-a-block program."

He grabbed a napkin from the plastic holder, reached for a pen from his shirt pocket, and began to scribble down his thoughts. He dictated as he wrote: "Here's what I think the Lord is asking us to do. Let's take the most violent neighborhoods in our city and break them down into twenty-home clusters."

We ended up calling them "parishes," based on Louisiana's long-standing county-line structure. He said, "I'm going to go before the church and ask for families to adopt each of these parishes, but I need somebody to head up the whole thing. This is where you come in, Brady. I'd like you to administer the entire program, to organize whatever needs organizing, and see it all through to the end. I need you to go into all these neighborhoods, be my eyes and ears on the ground, sort out the urgency for me, determining which blocks require our attention most. I need you to tell me where our people need to be and how we can position ourselves most strategically to help reduce gang activity and crime in our state."

I still have that napkin. That napkin meant the world to me because it was given to me on the day when one of my living heroes invited me into the game. The beloved pastor's vision for city renewal shapes my ministry still to this day.

So, he extended the offer, and of course I accepted. He *needed* me, after all. How I needed to be needed. This was an easy yes.

RUNNING TO SAVE MY HIDE

The first few weeks in my new role as the de facto kill-crime-not-each-other administrator were spent going on ride-alongs with various police officers who were accustomed to the high-crime beat. According to their assessment of things, the safest time of the week for me to be in these neighborhoods was from eight until noon on Saturday mornings, when gang lords were still fast asleep. Saturday, my only day off.

Saturday, it was.

During those car rides, my newfound police-force friends would point out various houses and say such things as: "That's where the twelve-year-old girl was raped last night." "Here's where that murder yesterday took place." "A couple of Bloods live there, a few Crips there." "That's where the shooting happened." "This sweet grandmother here has lost two grandkids to guns. She wants to move away, but where's she supposed to go?"

I didn't know these people yet, but their stories were tenderizing my heart. I wanted to rescue them, to save them, to deliver them from this sin-stained life. And so, with all the passion and energy I could muster, I began mapping out the most violent neighborhood, street by street by street, noting the most dangerous violators and most vulnerable residents. And then I came up with ideas for serving them both. When I finished mapping that first neighborhood, I began mapping the next. And when that one was completed, I started in on the third. On and on I went, organizing two hundred parishes in all. Our church eventually adopted four thousand homes, and I became the steward over them all.

Pam and I raised our hands—along with 199 other families—to "adopt" a block of these homes. And so, every Saturday morning, we'd make our way to Abbie Street, knocking on doors, meeting "our" families, and, as time went on, serving them, praying with them, loving them, and meeting their needs as best we could.

I would arrive early those Saturday mornings and teach outreach principles to all two hundred church families who'd come to serve, and then we'd disband to visit our adopted families. Then, several hours later, after those morning visits were completed, we'd reconvene and celebrate and tell stories of what God had done. By the time Pam and I got home, it would be two in the afternoon. So from eight in the morning until midafternoon, year after year after year, this is how my "day off" got spent.

It was a far cry from what Pam signed up for when she married me. During those first years of marriage, Pam probably envisioned lazy Saturday mornings, late breakfasts, a few hours to enjoy life as husband and wife. Instead, she got busyness, chaos, and a husband too distracted to see straight. Yes, she loved serving those folks on Abbie Street. And yes, she enjoyed being with me, even if we were busy. But she deserved better. She deserved more. She deserved better and more of *me*.

HOUSE IN FLAMES

For four straight years, I kept this pace, never stopping even to blink. In fact, whenever it seemed I might be able to slow my pace a bit, I let myself get roped into further busyness, which caused further strife at home. On one occasion, during those years when I had been coaching all those teams, driving the athletic bus, washing the uniforms—the whole bit—the day came when basketball season was over, meaning I could finally catch a break. The day after the season ended, the school's athletic director called all of the head coaches into his office and explained he had fired the track coach that morning—for good reason, according to him. Baseball season was in full swing, so the baseball coach couldn't help out. Spring football had already begun, so the football coach couldn't help out. Which left me. All eyes cut to me. "Brady," the AD said, "I need you to coach track. End of discussion."

In a split second, my long-awaited dream of being home at three thirty or four every afternoon vanished into thin air.

I informed Pam of my new role, and not long after that, I came home to find that my wife of five years had packed her bags. I think her exact explanation was: "If I'm going to be a single woman, I'd rather be single at my parents' house."

Admittedly, it wasn't my best day.

I was talking with a friend recently about this dark season from my past, and she asked, "Weren't there warning shots fired along the way?" (Translation: "Didn't you know what an idiot you were being?")

Yeah, I suppose the answer is yes—which proves it actually is possible to be too busy putting out other fires to notice your own house is going up in flames. My lovely and devoted wife would often ask if we could go on a date along the way, but who had time for that? A clear example comes to mind. Two weeks prior, on a rare Saturday when we didn't have parish ministry, Pam looked forward to spending time as a couple, just the two of us, with nothing on the agenda for an entire day. But that wasn't meant to be. I had been invited by a local soup kitchen to speak to their staff and guests, and because I didn't have any other obligations that day, I jumped at the opportunity to serve. It actually never occurred to me to invite Pam on a date or to plan "together time" for the day. It also never occurred to me to tell her of my plans at the soup kitchen.

That Saturday morning, I got dressed, grabbed a piece of toast, and headed for the door. I quickly pecked Pam on the cheek as I mumbled a bread-crumbed good-bye, which is when I noticed there was no return greeting from my wife. There was nothing but an icy stare. You know that stare, the one that tells you that a time bomb is about to go off? It's not a good look to get. Wordlessly, she conveyed her furor over my making plans without her for the day, and in response, I wordlessly conveyed my furor over her failing to understand how much my ministry mattered to me. When the icy stare did give way to actual words, Pam said, "You're not building God's kingdom. You're building the empire called Brady Boyd!"

THE TROUBLE WITH SEEKING MY OWN GLORY

Of course, my wife was right all along, despite my inability to see the cold, hard truth for what it was. In hindsight, I see that the problem for me back then was I was seeing so much fruit from all my hard work. I was saving the city, right? I was showing up, working hard, being celebrated left and right: "Brady, tell us another story!" my pastor would say to me in front of the church's eager Sunday morning congregation. "Come up here and tell us what you saw happen yesterday!" And so I would. I'd take the podium and explain how I'd seen a man in an adjacent neighborhood have his blind eyes literally healed, right before my own. Or how another guy's withered hand returned to normal while I held it, just like in biblical times. Or how a couple that had cussed us out week after week finally listened to the story of Christ. One woman—oh, this one blew me away—she was a *prostitute* when my wife and I met her, but she eventually surrendered her life to the Lord. Come on, now. Pam wanted me to walk away from all *this*?

I was in my glory, which should have been my first clue that something was amiss. It was my glory I was seeking. And it was my glory that I gained. But nothing seemed broken back then. I kept gulping down that sweet-tasting fruit, the fruit of all those harried weeks, followed by all those not-quite-relaxing days off.

Unfortunately, the taste didn't sit so well with Pam, and she thought it best to let me know. To her, I was a dead man walking. She'd already begun preparing my last meal.

I walked into our tiny house that night, saw Pam—disillusioned, angry, d-o-n-e done—and her packed bags, and experienced the lead weight in the bottom of my stomach; you know, the one that tells you all is not right in your world.

The Pam I'd married five years prior was gentle, calm, a lamb not a lion, a peacemaker not prone to provoke. But here, now, with those packed bags signaling her seriousness, I saw another woman emerge, a woman who refused to be taken for granted, a woman who would rather be single than be married and do life all alone. I may not have been supersmart, but there were signals even a dumb jock shouldn't have missed. "Pam," I said, my voice low and my words slow, "if you will stay here tonight—if you will agree not to leave tonight—I will walk in tomorrow and resign."

The red rims around her eyes told me she'd been crying all afternoon. "No, you won't," she challenged. "You won't."

I asked for twenty-four hours, to prove that I'd make good on my promise. And by that time the following day, I had resigned every last role. I told the principal that I would finish out the school year, but that at that point, I was done. She was floored, as was everyone else who discovered what I'd done. I had taken our girls' team to the

29

state semis, where they played in front of five thousand people, and had been voted coach of the year for our district.

Suffice it to say, I was invested in my endeavors. And then one day, I quit. "How can you not want to coach anymore?" people would say, as though I'd decided to stop being human. In my heart, I knew the answer: I did want to keep coaching. I just wanted to keep being married more.

A LONG-AWAITED TURNING POINT

I continued to work hard in the years that followed, but with a loving wife and then, eventually, two small children at home, I gladly kept my schedule in check. They were my magnetic north, my motivation to stay healthy and whole. And I did, largely. I went to work in radio, making stagnant stations profitable. Then in a strange turn of events, I was invited to enter a new role, that of pastor, first of a small church in Texas, then to a not-so-small church in Texas called Gateway.

Fast-forward to 2007. New Life Church in Colorado Springs came calling, wondering if I'd be interested in being the new senior pastor. The founding pastor, Ted Haggard, had resigned his post after a moral failure, and the church was wounded and raw.

I didn't think I had a shot after that first interview with the search committee, but as weeks passed, I received word that, among the candidates, I was in the top ten, and then the top four, and then, assuming the congregation was amenable to the idea, that I'd be the "new guy."

In those first months at the helm of New Life, I remember sticking to my rhythmic routine. Senior staffers used to mock me for how much I rested, in fact. Once, I pulled aside one of the other pastors and asked, "So, what do people say about me behind my back? What's the big 'Pastor Brady' inside joke?"

He didn't even hesitate: "It's that if we ever can't find you, you're probably busy taking a nap somewhere."

This probably wasn't meant as a compliment, but I took it as one. To me, it meant I'd been released from the desperation that is death row. I'd finally learned to slow down.

During those first few years at my new church, I worked hard at rest, and I encouraged everyone who would listen to join me. At the close of Sunday morning services, I'd tell our congregation to go home and take a nap. I forced all our long-term staff members to take six-week sabbaticals—and to *actually rest* while they were gone. To various ministry department leaders, I'd say, "Speed of the leader, speed of the team; the reason your staff is exhausted and cranky is because you are behaving the very same way."

To my credit, this lasted awhile—for just over four years, I think. And this was a necessary thing: our church had been through a sex scandal (not pertaining to me, I should clarify) and a deadly shooting, followed by months and months of heart-wrenching devastation and grief. It was tough going there for a while, validating my early suspicions when the search committee declared me the new pastor that I was actually coming to Colorado to preside over a long, slow death. New Life had been a marvelous church for nearly three decades, but even the sturdiest of congregations can't survive a scandal *and* a shooting; those churches become used-car lots. So while I kept my optimism close at hand, as I made my way to Colorado, I wondered if I'd actually signed up to serve as a hospice nurse—somebody to provide a little dignity while the one who lays dying fades from this thing called life.

The numbers initially proved me right: after two murders on our campus, attendance flagged, tithes declined, and morale took an understandable hit. In many ways, we were a healthier bunch than we'd ever been, thanks to the sane pace I insisted we prize, but even a well-rested church ceases to flourish when people and money go away. I was right in the middle of bracing myself for our inevitable demise when the miraculous happened: the deceased came back to life.

YOU KNOW PEACE WHEN YOU FIND IT

In the summer of 2011, on the heels of that rhythmic four-year run, I admitted myself into a Denver hospital, took a deep breath, and waited to be prepped for surgery. According to the cardiovascular experts who advised my mom when I was a young boy, the congenital heart condition I was graced with would require several interventions throughout my life. This was one of those interventions: valve replacement, a little spring-cleaning, perhaps insertion of a defibrillator just for grins.

I was terrified. And also strangely at peace.

Looking back, I see that the nine weeks surrounding that surgery were some of the best weeks of my life. The days leading up to and following the wild ride of having my chest cavity split wide open afforded me unprecedented opportunities for rest. And rest I did. I had no choice in the matter, really. I was so weakened by the process that my body *insisted* I slow down. It has been said, "Pain comes alive when it talks—even more so when it cries."[1] This is how so many of us find rest, isn't it? We don't find it at all; more the case, it finds us. Wayne Muller wrote, "If we do not allow for a rhythm of rest in our overly busy lives, illness becomes our Sabbath—our pneumonia, our cancer, our heart attack, our accidents create Sabbath for us."[2] My heart surgery wasn't necessarily medically connected to the stress I chose to bear in my life, but spiritually, I saw it for what it was: finally, a chance to rest.

During the eight days I was in the hospital, I pretty much lived in my bed. The sole instruction I'd been given by docs was to "rest … and then rest some more." I took only a few infrequent and poorly executed strolls up and down the hallway outside my room.

My Dallas Mavericks were vying for the NBA championship that year, and luckily for me, there was a little television at my bed-side. Late one night, probably as a result of my euphoria over the success of the Mavs, I was still lying there awake at two o'clock in the morning. The blinds on my window were raised, and through my fourth-floor window, I spotted a full moon in all its glory, a great big ball of bright light. I lay there quietly, taking it in, talking to God while staring at that moon. When was the last time I'd done that? Had I ever been so at peace in my life during an insomniac moment such as this? The reality was that I had absolutely nothing to do the next day, nothing to do but rest. And so I just breathed. I sank deeper into my bed. I talked to God. Most important, I didn't fret. Eventually, I fell asleep.

I returned to my leadership responsibilities weeks later but took things slow for a while. I preached while perched on a stool, for instance. I kept my meeting schedule light. I left the office early every afternoon so I could go home and take a leisurely walk.

Interestingly, during those slow-going weeks and months following my surgery, my preaching improved. My leadership improved. My ability to think even improved. My surgeon explained that the leaky valve I'd been living with had been taking a hit on my energy level, and now that we'd replaced it, I'd see an uptick in stamina and drive. But I suspect there was something more spiritual at work. I think things were turning around for the better because the point person had learned to rest.

Or had I?

For the two full years since my surgery, New Life has had the Midas touch. We've watched everything we've put in our hands turn to kingdom gold. Attendance is soaring, giving is increasing, and involvement is at an all-time high. There is growth. There is energy. There is momentum. There is fun.

Simultaneously, my "rhythmic living" has absolutely gone down the tubes. I've always said the greatest risk to restfulness is success; now more than ever, I stand by that claim. Failure invites us to pause, to regroup, to take stock, and to *rest*. In the sorrow, in the pain, in the deep, dark valleys we tend to find ourselves in, we are humbled, we are pensive, and we are undone. As a result, we tend to stop. But when we're soaring up with the eagles? Well, who wants to come down from that?

Here's what happened to me: while I was crouched over, offering what I thought was a little merciful mouth-to-mouth to a dying church, the thing had the audacity to sputter, to come to life, to take off and run. How was this even possible? I thought we'd never see success again at New Life Church. I know what success looks like; at Gateway, we went from one hundred fifty people to twelve thousand in seven years. *That* looked like success. That looked like what happens in a church where there have been no scandals, no shootings, no struggles just to stay alive. But New Life? Who would have predicted she would rise from the ashes and live?

But I liked how success felt. I didn't want to unplug. I didn't want to relax. The last thing I craved was rest. To allow any semblance of space to come between our church's newfound success and me was to cause the undesirable effects of withdrawal. I had become an addict again, an addict in search of a fix—a speed-and-wild-success junkie who never wanted to come down. And so I didn't. I stayed up, up, up, for two years straight, flying high on the wings of achievement, soaking up the opportunities, the attaboys, the hope. Truly, when things are shiny and wonderful, there is no better role in the world than that of a megachurch pastor. But I ran too hard, too fast, too far, and I neglected the rhythms I said mattered most. I allowed the joyride to carry me away, to cause me to drift toward frantic and frail. This makes sense, doesn't it? Because we never drift toward restoration and we never drift into a place of peace.

Eventually, I melted down. Again. Hello, death row, it's me, Brady. Back for another stay.

SOMETIMES, REST FINDS US

Around the same time I realized I'd forsaken all the restfulness I'd worked so hard to attain, a pastor friend of mine resigned from his church. He was asked to resign, actually. In a turn of events that seems tragically cliché, he'd engaged in a sexual relationship with a young woman on his staff. For thirty-plus years he had founded and then formed this fantastic, thriving congregation, and in one swift move, he tossed it all away—his life, his marriage, his credibility with his kids, his future, their future, the whole deal. He threw it all away.

After the dust settled, I contacted a member of his team, and here is what he said to me privately: "He didn't know how to get off the roller coaster." So my friend had decided to *make* it stop. Of course he didn't do this consciously; it's not as though he woke up one morning and said, "Gee, today I think I'll wreck my entire life." No, something in his psyche just knew the ride had to stop. And because my friend didn't know how to seek out healthy rhythms on his own, he made decisions that would utterly force him to rest. This is how so many of us find rest, remember? Sometimes, it just finds us.

It occurs to me that this could be why roller-coaster rides never last for more than about two minutes. We simply can't take the adrenaline surge for much longer than that. I think this is true in life outside the amusement park as well; we've got to learn how to stop the ride, without sabotaging our very lives.

It has been seven months since my friend left ministry, and while he hates what happened—the choices he made, the lives he wrecked, the stained reputation that will forever be attached to his name—he admits that he has never been as healthy in his adult life as he is today. It took a scandal that rocked his world and the loss of everything he had held dear in order to finally learn how to slow down, to tend to his soul, and to rest.

It's a story that shakes me to my core. I don't want to be that guy. I want to learn the easy way, not the hard way—from here on out, anyway. I want to live as a person of rest. I want to be drawn in by the restfulness of Christ, by the rhythms he has asked me to prize.

BREAKING BUSY

To begin breaking your addiction to busy, take a few minutes to engage with the "Breaking Busy" challenges at each chapter's end. Give yourself grace as you go; changing long-standing patterns isn't easy, but, boy, is it worth it in the end. Your family, your friends, your colleagues, and even your own soul will thank you for investing time and energy in charting a new and healthier course for your life.

Challenge #1: Acknowledge Unhealthy Rhythms
Even the healthiest and holiest people have some rhythms that don't serve them well. Maybe you, too, need to chronically sign up for more than what your soul's capacity will allow, and perhaps you also need to be needed. Maybe you consistently neglect to carve out time to spend with God each day, or you "come down" from a workweek in a less-than-stellar way. Think about your own life—your own daily ebbs and flows. What rhythms aren't serving you well? Which could stand to be adjusted or altogether removed? On a sheet of

paper or in your journal, jot down the unhealthy rhythms that come to mind. Don't worry yet with how to change them; we'll deal with that in a later chapter. For now, simply get them down in writing so that they're top of mind as you read on.

Challenge #2: Accurately Count the Cost

Next, beside each rhythm you've noted, record the toll each one is taking on your life. For example, if you don't spend time daily reading the Scriptures or praying, you may feel your days lack purpose or that a pervasive spirit of anxiety hovers over you like a cloud. Or, if you tend to relax after a long workweek by drinking too much or neglecting quality time with your family, you may feel disconnected from those you love most. If you struggle to count the cost for each unhealthy rhythm you jotted down, try asking the question, "What would be working better in my life if I could shift this rhythm from unhealthy to healthy?" The answer to that question just might reveal to you what it is you presently lack.

2

RESTLESS BODIES, RESTLESS MINDS

I love a broad margin to my life.
—Henry David Thoreau

I do, too, Henry, but who has time for that?
—Brady

SUFFERING FROM THE "AND THEN" SYNDROME

I'm sitting in my office at the church as I work on this chapter. It's a good-sized office with thick walls, carpeted flooring, and a wooden door that shuts. In other words, it should be a place of peace and quiet. It was designed for peace and quiet. Which is a good thing, because this is where I study for sermons, where I hold important meetings, and where I write. But too often, while I'm sitting in here, in this supposed place of peace and quiet, this is the thought that races through my mind: *I wish I had some peace and quiet.*

Interesting, isn't it? I can't find peace of mind in a place solely dedicated to my peace of mind.

There's a reason for this. Most days, I step inside my office ready to get some work done. I shut the door behind me, figuratively closing off the rest of the world. I get comfortable at my desk, fire up my laptop, and ready my mind and my fingers for the task at hand. Peace. Quiet. Yes, now I can make some strides.

And then I think, *I'd like to listen to some music,* and so I launch my Pandora app.

And then I remember a friend telling me about a terrific TED Talk he heard, and I search for the file online.

And then I think of the recent tornadoes in Oklahoma, and I decide to run a local news feed in the background.

And then I wonder about my "friends'" Facebook updates and decide to scroll through them just for a sec.

And then I check to see if anyone has retweeted the clever tweet I tweeted last night.

And then while I'm on the web, I Google my name, which is never a wise thing to do. The time-wasting tangent I then pursue lasts twenty minutes at least.

And then—look!—my buddy in Texas sends me a YouTube link, explaining that this is the funniest thing since the video on the evolution of dance. And sucker that I am, I click on it, I watch it, and I'm actually dumber in three minutes flat.

And then I hear the people outside my office chatting and laughing and carrying on, and I wonder what they're doing. So I just pop my head out there and see.

A really smart psychologist wrote a book about people like me, people who suffer from "and then" syndrome. He refers to us as the "frazzled."[1]

It sounds cute and cuddly, doesn't it? Sort of like a harmless, furry Muppet.

It's not cute and cuddly. It's deadly to both body and mind.

Frazzle is when you can't hold a thought in your mind for two seconds before it disappears into thin air. Frazzle is when you can't concentrate on A because you start thinking about B and C. Frazzle is when there's a washing machine in your head, and it's permanently set on spin cycle. Frazzle is when you can't find peace and quiet in the quietest, most peaceful place.

Sadly, for people like me anyway, those who insist on staying frazzled, we ultimately fizzle out.

In his groundbreaking book *Adrenaline and Stress*, Dr. Archibald Hart supports this idea with results from the research he's done. "People in a hurry don't allow time for their complex bodies and minds to become revitalized," he wrote. "So they accelerate the wear and tear of their bodies. There is no time for contemplation or even meditation. Anxiety increases and they lose perspective on their problems because they don't have time to think constructively. This makes them even more stressed and less able to cope with the strains of life, thus exacerbating the stress of life.

"In short," he goes on, "people of our time are showing signs of physiological and psychological disintegration because they are living at warp speed."[2]

"Disintegration" isn't a good way to articulate my aspirations in life. Is it a good way to articulate yours? Especially for those of us who say we love God, falling apart and fizzling out aren't exactly the goal.

I should mention here that I'm referring to those of us who are *choosing* frazzle as our MO. Clearly, so many men and women are not, such as those who have been handed exhausting situations. I think of friends of mine who have a special-needs child or friends who have decided to take in an elderly parent or friends who have chronic health issues of their own. I think of those whose spouses are on tours of duty; and those who work three part-time jobs every day, just to make ends meet; and those who have six kids, all less than six years old, whom they need to care for and love well and feed. Whenever people who are involuntarily frazzled seek out my advice, I work with them on reducing chaos, while recognizing that in many cases, a certain amount of chaos is going to be part of the equation for a while.

But back to my loving diatribe aimed at people like me, people who tend to willingly sign up for craziness, who tend to intentionally live chaotic lives: we are not doing as well as we think.

WHAT THE WEARY WILL DO

I'm a man who loves God. I love worshipping God, following God, and hearing from God through prayer. But what occurs to me is that it's more than a little difficult to pay attention to *God's* thoughts, when I can't even pay attention to my own. Throughout the normal course of my days, if someone were to ask, "Brady, what are you thinking about?" I'd actually have to pull back for a minute and think about what I was thinking about, which tells me I wasn't being very intentional with those original thoughts.

This would be fine, except that the Bible says it's not fine. Instead, the Bible tells me to "take captive every thought to make it obedient to Christ."[3] And to "love the Lord [my] God with … all [my] mind."[4] And to "have the same mindset as Christ Jesus."[5] And to think about things that are true and noble and pure.[6] And to "set [my mind] on things above, not on earthly things."[7] And to actually count God's thoughts as "precious,"[8] something I'm rarely able to do. To count God's thoughts as precious assumes I am first even aware of his thoughts. I'm pretty sure someone as perpetually distracted as I am isn't scoring any victories on this front.

I keep thinking about this idea, how too often I'm not in touch with what I'm thinking. The last few days I've been testing myself, pausing periodically throughout my day and asking, "Brady! Quick! What are you thinking about?"

Which has led me to an early conclusion: what I spend the vast majority of my time thinking about is not what I'm supposed to be thinking about.

I crave rest for my body, yes. But more immediately, and for reasons that are now obvious, I crave it for my mind.

I want to know what God is thinking. I want to know what he is thinking about my spiritual development. I want to know his thoughts on my wife and on my kids. On my colleagues. On my friends. On my neighbors. On our world at large. How can I possibly serve his restoration agenda in this world when I can't get a bead on his thoughts? I do want to know his thoughts, but that will require margin, space, and time.

Margin, space, and time are things I desperately want these days. I know I'm not alone.

Ultimately, every problem I see in every person I know is a problem of moving too fast for too long in too many aspects of life.

Every problem.

And I see a lot of problems.

Sex and money problems in marriage come back to the issue of speed. (How eager for intimacy are you when you're exhausted at the end of yet another grueling workday?)

Negligence in business practices comes back to the issue of speed.

Friendships that aren't quite clicking can usually point to the culprit of speed.

Speed is the single greatest threat to a healthy life, and it is also our greatest defense. We think if we can keep going, keep moving, and keep plowing ahead, our consciences won't have time to catch us because "ha-ha!" we'll already be long gone.

And the reality is this approach actually works. But only for a time. In his book *Sabbath*, author Wayne Muller wrote: "I had put a quote from Brother David Steindl-Rast on my bulletin board. Life, he said, was like the breath: We must be able to live in an easy rhythm between give and take. If we cannot learn to live and breathe in this rhythm … we will place ourselves in grave danger."[9] Maybe even the literal grave.

LEARNING FROM THE UNRESTED BEST

Three weeks ago, I received word that one of my closest friends had been hospitalized during an international trip. He had flown halfway around the world to speak at a high-profile pastors' conference, but toward the end of his trip, his stress level took him down.

He was in his hotel room the night before he was due to speak when a throbbing migraine struck. Everything seemed to make it worse: movement, light, sound. And so he lay there in the quiet darkness, willing it to go away. But it didn't; it only got worse.

He called the cell number he had for the host pastor and asked if there was a doctor in the man's congregation who might be willing to stop by. The pain was making him dizzy and nauseated, and my friend's anxiety level was rising by the hour. What could possibly be wrong with him? What could bring on sharp pain like this?

An hour later, a doctor from the church made his way to my friend's hotel room. The doc did an examination and prescribed some meds, and then before leaving gave him specific instructions on the drugs and a shot in the arm of something intense. But evidently the painkiller he'd just administered didn't sit too well with my friend. Within minutes, my buddy's stomach began bleeding, and in a few hours, he'd lost four pints of blood. The average adult has approximately just ten pints to start with; the situation was turning serious, and fast.

After an ambulance ride, three days in a foreign hospital, and a touch and go trip back home, my friend survived. But not without being changed by the experience. His regular doctor here in the States ordered a stress reduction ... *immediately*. Evidently my buddy's adrenal system was so used and abused—what, for going on thirty years?—that his body had begun to shut down. The only thing that would make him healthy again was rest, a whole lot of concentrated rest.

I talked to my friend after he'd returned home, and over the phone, I could nearly hear him shaking his head at himself. "I've been running too fast," he said. "Too fast, for way too long."

Involuntarily my cheeks burned in recognition. I had spent nearly two decades running too fast for too long ... would that damage catch up to me someday too?

A handful of elders from the church where he pastors banded together and formed something of an arbitration committee that would help him streamline his schedule for the foreseeable future—begging off of current obligations and declining speaking opportunities that had not been accepted yet. But in one sense, this intervention was too little too late. Frightening damage had already been done.

We love and admire and follow these leaders because of the great gains we believe them to make, and yet we unwittingly cheer them right over the cliff, wishing them well as they crash to the ground.

Even now, as I'm typing this paragraph, a tweet appears on my feed from a pastor I really should quit following. It reads, and I quote: "Taped a TV show. Wrote a new talk. Ran five miles. All on my day off. What did you do on YOUR day off?" No rest for the weary, right? We're learning from the unrested best.

We owe one another better than this. We owe one another rest.

But what does real restfulness look like for ones so addicted to hard-core/fast-paced lives? Where do we even begin?

BREAKING BUSY

Challenge #1: Fess Up

Look back at the list of unhealthy rhythms you made at the close of the last chapter, and also at what each of those rhythms is costing you in terms of quantity and quality of life. Now, take things one step further by logging a few things that weariness has caused you to do along the way. Have you cut corners in business practices? Shortchanged your children the devoted attention from you they deserve? Allowed key relationships to slip into maintenance mode? Something else? Ask God to show you what weariness has instigated in your life, and record the revelations you receive.

Challenge #2: You, in Ten Words

Now to a cheerier exercise. On a fresh sheet of paper, number a list one to ten. Beside each number, write down an adjective you wish to be true of you. Maybe you are sick of running yourself ragged and long to be peaceful. Or maybe you are fed up with shortchanging your kids and want to be engaged or present. Perhaps you see clearly how far you've run from God and want to re-up your commitment to being righteous. Whatever the dream looks like, try to describe it in ten adjectives.

3

DISTRACTION VERSUS DEVOTION

He who can no longer pause to wonder and stand rapt
in awe is as good as dead; his eyes are closed.

—Albert Einstein

PERILOUS PROGRESS

Matthew Sleeth wrote, "We are a hydroponic society, fed by the drip irrigation of electronic social networks,"[1] and I happen to think he's right. He's right, and he's right for good reason: technology *is* fascinating, and smartphones *are* amazing. It was only a few decades ago that the only telephone I had access to was a rotary-dial clunker in my parents' living room. I'm sure many of you remember those. If your number had a bunch of nines in it, nobody ever called you, because it was just too much work, pulling that little wheel all the way around again and again. My aunt and uncle lived across the street, and my family shared a party line with them. If the phone rang once, it was for us; if it rang twice, it was for them.

But to my point: look at the progress we've made! On my smartphone today, I have instant access to pretty much everyone I've ever known or could ever want to know, via Facebook, Twitter (@pastorbrady ... not that I'd ever self-promote), and a phone that can call anywhere in the world. I have weather updates, including live Doppler images for any city on planet earth. I have a camera and a thousand of my recent photos, right here, ready to show you (Instagram: @pastorbrady67). I have my contact database, complete with people's physical addresses, email addresses, phone numbers, spouses' names, kids' names, company names, company addresses, and birthday information. I have feeds from news and sports sites that keep me apprised of interesting goings-on. I have texting capability, which allows me to get questions answered or pass along urgent information to those in my relational circle in the span of about three seconds. I have one-click access to the World Wide Web, which can tell me anything I don't already know. Heck, I even have a Bible on here, in every translation known to humankind. In fact, I can "follow" the globe's most noteworthy pastors, receiving their verse-of-the-day installments long before my alarm clock sounds, and pretty much check off my "quiet time" to-do with a sixty-second scroll through my tweets.

With my phone handy, I never have to think. It tells me what to think. I don't even have to wonder what to think about, because it tells me all the time. There is seemingly nothing this thing can't do, and all with just a little more than a swipe of my thumb. Which is why I'm so attached. Why we are so attached.

I got to work a few days ago and realized I'd left my phone at home. The all-out search that proved futile and the ensuing overwhelming angst I experienced were significant. I think I was more distraught than if I'd misplaced one of my children. *How am I going to get through this day without my phone?* Fortunately, I found it in my computer bag. But not before I was reminded how utterly obsessed I am with my phone. I check that thing a hundred times a day (current research says it's actually a hundred and fifty[2]), swiping for the time, swiping for the weather, swiping to make a call. Most days, the biggest crisis I face has to do with keeping my cell phone charged. I think this is what we refer to as a first-world problem.

In addition to my handy smartphone, I have a giant television set at home that allows me access to more than one hundred channels, and there is a stack of well over two hundred DVDs just to its side. I justify this over-the-top investment by saying to myself, "Well, our family never goes out for entertainment, so we need something here at the house." It's true. But is being a gear hound okay?

I've admitted that all this gear is very, very cool. And it is. But here's what I'm learning is not so cool: becoming more fascinated with my stuff than with God.

This is a problem not because I say so, but because God does. "Come to me," he said in Matthew 11:28, "all you who are weary and burdened, and *I will give you rest*" (NIV; emphasis mine).

When God said that rest is found in him, he means that *rest is found in him*. Translation: real rest is found nowhere else. Recently I heard a pastor in Maryland talking about the difference between amusement and rest. We tend to do one better than the other, and the one we do well is *not* rest. Case in point: last year my family and I went to Disney World for a full week, and I came back more exhausted than before I left. And I was *really* tired when we took off. I may have escaped the stressors of daily life, but had I even rested at all? This is what God is hinting at here, that restfulness is tethered to the state of our souls.

We acknowledge that a healthy heart rhythm is critical for maintaining good health. A steady heartbeat is kind of necessary, right? What we are slower to admit is that our souls require rhythm too. "All of us are aware that a healthy heart and regular daily and yearly rhythms are essential for health," wrote Dr. Christine Sine. "We also know that if our heartbeat is irregular then we need to see a physician for a checkup. Most of us, however, are unaware of the spiritual rhythms that are *just as crucial to our health and well-being.* Since our lives are increasingly disconnected from the rhythms of God's world, we do not hear the underlying whisper of God's heartbeat that is meant to sustain us, and we are unaware of the symptoms that should alert us to our growing ill health"[3] (emphasis mine).

She's right, you know. We don't hear the "underlying whisper of God's heartbeat," most likely because we've always got wired buds in our ears.

So when God says to us, "Come to me, and I will give you rest," we don't respond.

God tries again: "Lay your burdens down, children. Walk with me, and your walk will be burden-free." Again, we don't respond.

God says, "I want you to be fascinated not with trinkets, but with *me.*" Still no response.

Ever patient and ever persistent, God goes for it a fourth time: "Slow down. Look up. Linger here with me."

We think we hear something. Wait. Was that the voice of God? We glance skyward and say, "Huh? God? Was that you? What's 'linger'?"

But before he has a chance to reply, we hear subtle *dings* from our phones—alerting us to new text messages. Then we can't help but move our thumbs across our phones. Score one for the Enemy of our souls.

PURSUING A CALM AND QUIET SOUL

The world promises peace to us, but whatever nanosecond of restfulness or relief it offers is fragile, elusive, and circumstantial. It is also self-maintained: we must constantly find it, produce it, and keep it going, which causes us to work against what we seek. In reality, this isn't peaceful at all. It's the very opposite of peace. What we're craving is real-deal rest, rest that flows from the inside out. We're dying for this type of solace; how we wish we could simply stop.

Which brings me to the usefulness of lollygagging.

My son, Abram, is fifteen now, and one of our favorite things to do together is hang out at night in the hot tub behind our house. The Boyd home is situated on the Palmer Divide, a ridge north of Colorado Springs that has spectacular views in every direction. From any seat in the hot tub, you can see expansive flatlands to the east, a crush of ponderosa pines to the south, and crazy-bright stars overhead. It's surreal. It's *fantastic*. It's our refuge most every night.

Abram probably enjoys these times because it feels adventurous to be sitting outside in a tub of water with snow falling all around. Plus, despite what some parents report about the teenage years, Abram still relishes time with his dad. He loves it when he has me all to himself.

I, on the other hand, enjoy the times for different reasons. For me, these are some of the only unrushed, unrestricted conversations I have with my son. It seems as though in life there is always a clock—always a place to be, a start time, a stop time, a deadline, an obligation, a frantic "Hurry up! Let's go!" as everyone is herded out the door.

But not so in the hot tub. In the hot tub, there is no clock. There's warm water, a wide sky, and a kid with a thousand questions on his mind. Along the way I've bought Abram cool toys, taken him on exciting trips, and given him scores of interesting opportunities to pursue. But maybe the best investment I've ever made is showing up with open ears and an open mind—being present with him.

Ten or twenty years from now, when Abram is a grown man, what I'll miss more than anything are these hours spent fully engaged with him. Shooting the breeze. Lollygagging. Hanging out, father and son. I think God wishes for the same thing. A little lollygagging, a little engagement with his kids. It is God's presence that quiets our souls. It is God's presence that calms us down.

This "presence" thing—let me stay with this for a moment. I want you to think about two people in your life, the first being someone who seems preoccupied every time you're around them. You and I both have someone like this in our lives, someone who never quite seems to be listening as you talk, who never quite seems to be fully present when you get together for a cup of coffee, who never quite seems to pay attention when you honestly answer whatever question he just asked. This is the person who says, "So, what were your plans again for this weekend?" forty-five minutes into a lunch date because he wasn't listening when you answered that question the first time, forty minutes ago. Or the person who takes a call on his cell halfway through your emotional explanation of how your struggling teenager is doing these days and explains away the indecency by saying, "Oh! You've gotta hold that thought. I've been waiting all morning for this guy's call!"

Okay, so you have that person's face in mind?

Now, think about the most peaceful person you know. Maybe it's your spouse. Or your mom. Or a sibling or colleague or friend. For me, it's my longtime ministry mentor, Tom Lane. After my dad died nearly a decade ago, Tom became my father figure, and his easy confidence, his strong self-concept, and his deeply rooted passion for living like Christ instantly made me a better person. Tom is at peace, in every sense of the word. He is at peace in his work, in his family life, in his walk with Jesus, and in his world. And this peace is absolutely contagious. I come away from time spent with Tom feeling as though I've been gulping extra amounts of oxygen. My spirits are lifted, my soul is settled, and my sense of optimism is restored.

Interestingly, I've found that most people tend to think of God as the first type of person, someone who is perpetually preoccupied, who doesn't really have time for them. We race into his presence, toss a few prayer bones his way, and rush on to the next thing on our agendas, hoping something good or godly got attached to us, which will then carry us through our day.

But this isn't at all how God works. God is not merely a peaceful person; God, in fact, is peace. When we sit in God's presence, we're sitting in the presence of peace. And when we sit there—actually stay there, quiet, still—we come away breathing differently. We come away with steadied souls. From there, astoundingly, we can become people of peace. We can become more like God.

This is why God's invitation is so profound, the invitation to come to him to find our rest: he can actually deliver on what he promises, something the world never will be able to do.

I want this type of restfulness. I want to say yes to this.

We slow down—to rest, to contemplate, to lollygag with God—because *slow* can pay serious dividends, for our bodies, for our minds, and for our souls.

GIVING A NEW RHYTHM A TRY

On the night at the hospital when I woke and couldn't go back to sleep, days after my massive heart surgery, I felt a little like I was lollygagging with God. I didn't turn on the TV. I didn't crack open a book. I didn't even fret. I simply lay there, in the presence of my Lord. Totally unproductive. Totally inefficient. And also totally, and astoundingly, at peace. Granted, I was somewhat of a captive audience, there in a hospital bed with scores of wires and tubes attached to every square inch of my body. But despite my captivity, I enjoyed our time together. I enjoyed simply sitting in the presence of God.

It happened again recently, this swell of contentment, this sense of being delighted by the presence of God. Several weeks ago, I was asked to preach at a church in Charleston, South Carolina, for their Saturday evening and Sunday morning services. And with uncharacteristic deference to the state of my sagging soul, I decided to fly in a day early and simply spend time with God. To withdraw. To retreat. To give a new rhythm a try for once.

This scheme required more than simply booking a flight for Friday instead of Saturday. In addition, I would need to stand my ground and protect my margin in half a dozen ways: "No, I can't make the dinner Friday night"; "No, I also can't make the breakfast Saturday morning"; "No, I don't need someone from the church staff to show me around town Saturday afternoon"; and on and on it went. I appreciated all the well-meaning offers I received, truly, but they were all potential saboteurs of my Sabbath state of mind. It's tempting for extroverts such as I to believe that these little yeses don't matter, that they don't add to much in the end. But in fact they do. I love how Wayne Muller put it:

> This one little conversation, this one extra phone call, this one quick meeting, what can it cost? But it does cost, it drains yet another drop of our life. Then, at the end of days, weeks, months, years, we collapse, we burn out, and cannot see where it happened. It happened in a thousand unconscious events, tasks, and responsibilities that seemed easy and harmless on the surface but that each, one after the other, used a small portion of our precious life.[4]

I took Wayne's advice in South Carolina. And after enjoying a totally uneventful, totally obligation-free Friday night, I woke Saturday morning to still more hours of unscheduled time. I couldn't help but smile. I tugged on shorts and a T-shirt, laced up my running shoes, found the nearest trailhead to my hotel, and took it, figuring I'd go wherever it went.

The trail wound its way through a picturesque downtown area and up into a dense patch of trees. Here, the gravel gave way to dirt, the trail narrowed, and I could hear the crash of Atlantic waves up ahead. Forty-five minutes into my trek, I found myself standing before a dilapidated park bench that was positioned underneath a one-hundred-year-old oak tree whose long arms waved over scores of tombstones marking lives lost in World War I.

I took a seat and stretched out my legs. I took in the beauty surrounding me, breathing in the ocean's breeze. Officially, I was accomplishing nothing. But great gains were being made for my soul. It was then my gaze landed on the name carved into the tombstone positioned closest to me. It was an eighteen-year-old who had been placed in that grave, a young man who hailed from a different time. There were no cell phones in his day, no video games, no email, no Facebook, no TV. I'm sure he found distractions somewhere, but I had to wonder if it was easier to stay focused back then.

I also wondered what he might say to me, if he could send me a message here and now. Would he tell me to treasure the days I have, because life may end sooner than I think? Would he tell me to slow my pace, to practice presence, to quit multitasking my hours away?

I peered out over the ocean, taking in the layers of green, turquoise, and navy blue. The splendor of it all. The thought occurred to me that I couldn't have done this ten years ago—taken this time, chosen this reprieve. I wouldn't have seen the point.

I conceded that I may still eat too fast, talk too fast, walk too fast, and in general live by the code that says faster beats slower every time, but at least I was making progress. I had actually withdrawn from my daily chaos and parked myself on this rickety bench, lollygagging, fascinated with God.

LIVING FASCINATED WITH GOD

Nearly every morning I am responsible for driving my daughter, Callie, to school. Her school is on my way to work, so it only makes sense for me to be the one to take her. Plus, it affords us some quality dad-daughter time. Except that Callie doesn't really "do" dad-daughter time. Sure, she rides along. And she stays awake. And she breathes. But in terms of really engaging, of actually participating in our chat, I keep the bar pretty low. She has taught me to keep it low.

As a result of my daughter's ... *pensiveness*, you might say, I tend to overtalk—you know, just to fill the void a little. A few months ago, when I first began writing this book, I decided to use a portion of our otherwise silent morning commute to practice living like a person at peace.

The route from our home to Callie's school involves two quick left-hand turns, followed by going up a hill and then down the other side of the hill, followed by an absolutely stunning view of Pikes Peak.

So, each morning, as Callie and I made our way to her school, I'd comment on the state of Pikes Peak. This obviously required my actually *looking* at the mountain, which represented marked progress for me.

"Wow! The peak sure looks majestic today," I'd declare. Or, "Callie, can you believe how the sun is reflecting off the peak this morning?" Or, "I'll never get used to the grandeur of that peak!"

A few weeks ago, Callie and I were in my truck en route to her school, and, as usual, I made two left-hand turns before going up the hill and then down the hill. During our descent, I caught sight of the mountain and couldn't help myself. "Callie! Do you realize it's the middle of May and there is still all that snow at the top of Pikes Peak?"

As usual, there was no reply. Well, no verbal reply, I should say. I cut my eyes to the right to be sure my daughter had heard my enthusiastic report, and in my periphery, I caught a dramatic eye roll as she turned toward the window and sighed.

Yet again, I couldn't help myself. "What?" I asked good-naturedly. "Why the rolling of the eyes?"

With no attempt at hiding her exasperation, she said, "Dad"— her voice was huffy and she gave a second eye roll—"you *always* have to say *something* about the peak." She let out yet another disgusted sigh and crossed her arms. "*Every. Single. Day.* You make some comment about the peak."

I grinned.

"Callie," I said in reply, "what's true about your dad is that he is absolutely fascinated with God. Or I want to be, anyway."

Still nothing from the passenger's seat.

I went on. "This is my way of practicing that fascination, Callie, of practicing being fascinated with God. He put that mountain there. He put that snow on that mountaintop. And he invited me to have a look. You gotta admit: that's pretty cool."

Callie still didn't say anything, but out of the corner of my eye, I detected a subtle grin.

The sermonette I wanted to preach for Callie—but because of my better parental judgment, I did not—was this: I don't experience much fear in life, but one fear I live with is that someday, in some way, I'll lose my fascination with God. I live with this fear because I've met this fear. I met it all those years ago when I was too distracted to be devoted to the one thing I said I loved most: God. And from firsthand experience, I can tell you that when one loses his or her fascination with God, there is nothing left to be fascinated with.

Go ahead. Give it a try for a day. Decide to not be fascinated with God's creation, with God's people, even with God himself, and I guarantee by the time you put your head on the pillow that night, you'll be disillusioned, depressed, and cast down. This world without God is ugly, and people without God are fools. Some of them are fools even with God, but assuming you are viewing them through a godly lens, you can see past their idiocy and give them grace.

Yes, I comment on the snowcapped mountain in front of us, and for a very good reason. I don't want to miss a thing.

BREAKING BUSY

Challenge #1: Ditch the Distractions

No surprise here: For one full day—twenty-four complete hours!—turn off your phone. Or the radio in your car. Or ESPN. Whatever it is that distracts you from staying fascinated with God, let that thing rest for a day. Worry not: you don't have to ditch the distractions for a lifetime. I'm just suggesting that by untangling yourself from them for a day, you may realize just how tangled up you are. Which is the first step toward making necessary change.

Challenge #2: Tell God What You Hope to Find

As you power down your phone, your iPad, or your TV, take a few minutes to write out a prayer to God. What do you hope to discover about him, about his creation, about his people, or about yourself as you engage in this one-day "distraction fast"? Maybe you want to hear his voice for the first time in a long time. Maybe you wish you could receive divine insight regarding a particular problem you've been facing. Maybe you hope to feel a sense of peace that has been lacking in your spirit for a while. Think through what you hope to find as you shut out distractions for a day, and then candidly tell God your thoughts.

PART TWO: DISCOVERY
Calm or Chaos: We Get to Choose

A bee is never as busy as it seems; it's just that it can't buzz any slower.

—Kin Hubbard

4

BEING WHO WE ARE

Don't just do something, stand there.

—Lewis Carroll

JUST LIKE THEM

The first time I experienced real restfulness in my spirit, it happened inadvertently. I was working at a church in the Dallas–Fort Worth area, in a role that felt pretty important. Although Southlake, Texas, was only five towns on the map from my previous Hereford residence, socioeconomically it was from here to the stars and back. A few years ago, *Forbes* magazine ranked the wealthiest suburbs in the country, and of course Southlake made the list. It topped the list, in fact, beating out the most affluent suburbs of New York, San Francisco, and Washington, DC.[1] Today, even in a down economy, median household income there hovers just below $200,000, which represents more than 20 percent growth from census data five years ago.[2] For a guy who grew up in less than lavish conditions, Southlake was a real eye-opener. On a near-daily basis, I enjoyed lunch with businessmen and pastoral staffers from our church and other churches in the area at restaurants I couldn't have even worked at as a young man, let alone eaten at. It was opulence and ostentation like nothing I'd ever known.

There was a lot to like about Southlake. People were so put together, so polished and sparkly clean, so different from dusty West Texas, not to mention from those murky Louisiana swamps. I spent my entire young-adult life there in Southlake trying ridiculously hard to impress the older men I knew. In my view, it was the older men in society who held the keys to money, prestige, and power—three things I really, really wanted. So, even though I was half their age, I began to talk like them, walk like them, work like them, act like them, and look like them. I wanted them to see me as older and more mature than I was, and so I focused a great deal of energy on becoming "that" put together: Just. Like. Them.

I used to look at other guys my age who were sowing their wild oats, rebelling against "the system," and blowing all their money and time, and think, *What fools. Can't they see they're jeopardizing their entire future?* No, I was far too ambitious to goof around playing games. My heart condition probably played a key role here. Docs had forecasted an abbreviated life for me, and I figured if the clock was ticking, I'd better cram in as much as I could as fast as I could before my limited time ran out. If that meant becoming a sixty-year-old at age thirty, then so be it. I'd carefully crafted a new persona and was committed to keeping it afloat. Who needed authenticity, when money, prestige, and power surely were about to be mine?

We do this, you know. We spin and whir and run and race and then, at last, look up from all that speed and see we've become someone we never wanted to be. Sir Walter Scott, of *Rob Roy* and *Ivanhoe* fame, started one of his poems this way: "Breathes there the man, with soul so dead ..." On this subject of running ourselves through insane paces in the name of impression management, his words pretty much say it all. Even in the eighteen hundreds, it must have been evident we can get caught up in stuff that doesn't matter in the end.

We're breathing, yes. But are our souls even remotely alive?

Last fall I had the privilege of spending a couple of days with Eugene Peterson at his home in Montana. He's a personal hero of mine, so it was time well spent. Ridiculously well spent, actually. I came away with more wisdom and insight than I could ever hope to excavate, but here's one thing he mentioned that I'll remember for a long, long time: He said, "I can go anywhere; I can do anything; I can buy anything money can buy. But you know what? I don't have the appetite for it. I'm content—here, and now, with this life." He waved an open palm around the living room, indicating his immediate surroundings, yes, but also his life in general.

Eugene Peterson lived in relative obscurity until he was sixty-five years old, which is when he published his paraphrase of the Bible, *The Message*. Millions of copies were soon sold, and he was famous in the span of a year. But the fame and the financial gain did not own him. That's what he was saying that day: "It's fine, but it doesn't own me."

In his book *Reversed Thunder*, Peterson said that when God's kingdom comes, we will have all we need. But as great as that reality will be, there is something greater still, which is that we will *only want exactly what we have*. We will live from that place called *enough*. By being content with what he had, by only wanting what he already had, Eugene was practicing future happiness. In his own way, he was ushering in a bit of heaven, right here on planet earth. He was practicing being alive in an eternal sense. His heart wasn't merely beating; his soul was alive as well.

DARING TO BE ME

What I refused to grasp during those early days at Gateway was that tucking myself behind a facade every day, making sure none of the "real me" could be seen, is terribly exhausting work. By allowing the shiny, successful people in my life to dictate my pace, instead of trusting God to take care of that role, I was unwittingly denying myself rest.

Letting ourselves be who we really are is a key step in living a life at rest. It is when we free ourselves from the inner vows we've made—the ones that keep us spinning, whirring, running, racing—that we take our first steps toward rest. When we allow ourselves to cease living by our self-imposed declarations of what we'll do and not do—*I will not be poor; I will not be insignificant; I will matter; I will make a name for myself; I will make my family proud; I will finish what I started; I will outshine my superstar brother; I will be a perfect mom and a perfect employee; I will look right and dress right and be the one to have it all*—we discover what real living is: nearness to Christ, newness in Christ, choosing to walk at his pace.

God began to reveal these truths to me while I was still on staff at Gateway, and the freedom I felt was overwhelming: *I could be me, and that's enough.* One tangible shift that occurred immediately had to do with the ministry schedule I kept. When I was consumed with keeping up with the older men on our staff, I often neglected the needs of my family for the sake of being present at events at the church. But being me—the "real me"—meant acknowledging the priority my wife and two young kids held in my heart. And so, from that moment forward, if something was going on at the church that I really didn't have to be part of, I'd beg off, explaining to my superiors that I had a prior commitment. Occasionally my colleagues would probe, and I'd have to explain that the "commitment" involved hanging out with my kids, both of whom were less than five years old at the time. One of the other pastors on staff used to razz me for this. "Must be nice to have a built-in excuse," he'd say with something approaching a sneer, to which I'd respond, "They're not an excuse. They're kids who crave time with their dad."

I couldn't blame him for giving me a hard time. For so long, I was the guy standing in judgment of anyone and everyone who didn't appear to be working as hard and as long as I did, people who had the audacity to take time off or call a workday complete as soon as their eight hours were up. When you need to be needed, you'll willingly sign up for slavery like that.

WE ARE SO VERY BUSY

Give this a try: The next ten people you see face-to-face, pose the question, "How ya been lately?" And then count how many times you hear this in response: "Busy. *Sooo* busy." I'm willing to bet you'll go ten for ten.

What's not discussed in these I'm-so-busy-it-would-blow-your-mind discussions is the motivation for all that busyness. I have a theory on this, which is that busyness is our means to impress. If I'm busy, then I'm important, and if I'm important, then you'll be impressed. Right? Don't you do this too? A buddy calls you up and asks about having lunch sometime soon, and instead of answering succinctly, you feel compelled to give him the rundown of your (very busy, very important) week. "Well, I've got an off-site all day Monday, I'm in wall-to-wall meetings on Tuesday, Wednesday is an extended morning session with the board, and Thursday—well, it's already in the tank!"

Seriously. Why couldn't you just say no? Or, at a minimum, why couldn't you say, "What a kind offer. You know, I could swing Friday this week. Or else would something early next week work for you?"

Here's why you can't say that: because that is not an impressive reply. And, boy, how we love to impress. "Busyness serves as a kind of existential reassurance, a hedge against emptiness," one author wrote. "Obviously your life cannot possibly be silly or trivial or meaningless if you are so busy, completely booked, in demand every hour of the day."[3]

We buy more house than we can afford, we elevate vacation stories to epic proportions, we proudly tout our stuffed-full schedules, and we refuse to let others see us rest. Oh, the things we do in the name of impression management. We all want to be important. We all want our little lives to count. And yet we're going about it in entirely the wrong way. All the posing and posturing and performing may help you hit the quota, win the award, and be the guy who saves the day. But in terms of encouraging the stuff of righteousness? It won't even get you to step one.

Jesus said that all our boasting may get us some things, but it won't get us the one thing we truly seek, which is the soul-filling love of our Father, the sense that we're acceptable as we are. "Everything in the world—the lust of the flesh, the lust of the eyes, and the pride of life—comes not from the Father but from the world" (1 John 2:16 NIV).

In the gospel of Matthew, we are told not to be like the hypocrites, who love to pray to be seen by people, who love to flaunt their spirituality and their superiority, who love to devote themselves to trying to impress. No, instead, Jesus says we are to work on the inner self, spending our energies developing things such as a gentle spirit, which, according to 1 Peter 3:4, is "of great worth in God's sight" (NIV).

A gentle spirit—something we humans can't cultivate on the go.

Along the way, my family and I sort of institutionalized the practice of ditching impression management and working toward a quiet, gentle spirit instead. Once a week, we'd hole away for an entire day with nothing on the agenda and nobody to impress. We would wake when our bodies were done sleeping, instead of being jolted by a blaring alarm. We'd ignore the hands on the clock and open our own hands to an unscheduled day. We'd eat when we got hungry, move when we got antsy, rest when we got weary, and let the day come to us instead of maniacally chasing it down. Smartphones weren't the rage yet, but desktop computers were, and we took pains to keep ours shut down, to experience life not virtually but firsthand, here, in real time. Mostly, we puttered.

We ambled. Once a week, beautifully, we took a long, slow stroll through our day. Evelyn Underhill once said, "Hurry and impatience are sure marks of the amateur."[4] If she's right—and I think she is—then once a week, we Boyds were total pros.

ON BEDHEAD DAYS, BE LAZY

"Bedhead days" we came to call them, these times of extricating ourselves from the clutches of busy and intentionally focusing on rest. We didn't have any rules on our bedhead days—in fact, rules would have mucked up everything. But if there were three guiding principles that emerged over time, they were *be lazy*, *be together*, and *give grace*.

Suffice it to say, the most obvious things I rested from on those bedhead days were the clock, the calendar, and the ever-pressing need to go, go, go. But just as important was my practice of resting from people's expectations of me. I've always been pegged as a "driver" personality, and as such, I have enjoyed being known as the action-oriented one, the can-do one, the solution-seeking one, the guy who is responsible and reliable and strong and generally in charge. I like all these roles because they convince me I'm bringing value to the world.

Surely you can relate.

Maybe you're the optimistic one or the one who always organizes social gatherings or the one who is great at fund-raising or the one who always remembers snacks. Maybe you're the sparkling conversationalist or the steady listener or the master of little-known facts or the bleeding heart. Whatever your role may be, you probably like playing that role. We tend to attach our self-worth to these roles, but on a bedhead day, it's time to lay them down. It's time to rest from our roles and bask in the fact that we're loved for who—not what—we are. This is a terrifying and also marvelous thing to do, by the way. I dare you to try it. Just for a few hours, lay down all the stuff others think about you, all the roles you're asked to play. See if that newfound nakedness suits you. I guarantee you'll relish your stripped-down state.

Every January our church engages in twenty-one days of prayer and fasting, as a way to kick off the New Year in a contemplative way. During week two of the endeavor this year, a dear woman approached me following one of the prayer meetings and asked if she could have a word with me. She is a longtime New Lifer, a faithful servant, and someone who has been nothing but encouraging to me since my first week on the job. But this time, her encouragement soared to new heights. She was several minutes into her monologue of praise regarding my preaching, my teaching, my leadership, and my general greatness as a human being, when I realized that she wasn't describing me at all. Sure, she was describing her ideal of me, but the description was not *me*.

When she finished her well-meaning speech, I thanked her for her graciousness and kindness, for believing the very best about me. But privately, silently, I told myself to take it for what it was: a compliment, and nothing more.

There are two traps I tend to fall into regarding other people's opinions of me. The first is the pride trap: I can take people's affirmations of me and use them to inflate my self-assessment, my worth. I can become prideful and boastful and haughty and self-righteous and be a total jerk to be around. Or, on the other end of the spectrum, I can use others' input as a performance bar I have to clear. I can let insecurity and the need to please eclipse everything else, and I can subsequently throw my energies at living up to the standard they've set for me.

Both of these traps were tempting landing spots as I listened to that sweet woman pour on the praise. But an interesting thing happened en route to one of those two miry pits: I stayed steady right there, in between. I received her compliment without letting it puff out my chest or deflate my self-concept. I took it for what it was and moved on. Interestingly, I had enjoyed a bedhead day the day before that conversation, and I firmly believe that because I had spent the previous twenty-four hours resting—yes, from the clock but also resting from people's expectations of me—I was able to respond with maturity and grace.

See if you find this to be true as you make strides toward living rhythmically: The more rested you are, the less you are driven by what others think of you. The more rested you are, the more you are driven by what God, alone, believes to be true. This is a magnificent place to be, because Scripture is clear that God's thoughts toward us are good.

This brings me to what all this rest is for. We rest not just to be caught up on sleep or to build up our immune systems or to keep our bones healthy and strong—although all these things do happen as a result. We also rest for a deeper purpose, the purpose of meditating on the things of God—his character, his creation, his "come to me" promise—the realest of real invitations to rest. Sleeping in. A long walk. Watching the wind blow by. A picnic lunch. Pushing your kid on a swing. Reading ten pages of a good novel. Savoring a piece of dark chocolate. Mowing your lawn slowly while listening to the Eagles' greatest hits. There are a thousand ways to push Pause on the rush, to inject a little lazy into even the craziest of weeks.

ON BEDHEAD DAYS, BE TOGETHER

A second guiding principle for us Boyds was easier to practice than the first: *be together*. We love to be together, so this was sort of a given in our lives already. But still, as weeks turned into months and months turned into years and our kids grew up and outgrew their need to be no more than six feet from Mom and Dad, it was important for us to reinforce the importance of togetherness.

Sometimes we're reminded the hard way, as was the case for one guy on board during the "Miracle on the Hudson" event.

In the middle of the afternoon on January 15, 2009, US Airways Flight 1549 took off from LaGuardia Airport in New York City, bound for Charlotte, North Carolina. It was supposed to be an uneventful flight, but three minutes into the plane's ascent, passengers realized they were in for a wild ride. The captain, Chesley "Sully" Sullenberger, came over the intercom with a three-word request: "Brace for impact."[5]

Evidently, upon takeoff, the plane had struck a flock of Canada geese, which took out both engines in one fell swoop. Air-traffic controllers directed the captain toward nearby Teterboro Airport in New Jersey, but there wasn't enough time to get there. Captain Sullenberger chose the nearest "runway" he could find to land the plane: the middle of the Hudson River.

As expected, the 150 passengers aboard the plane put their heads in their laps and began to pray. I don't know about you, but I'd be praying too. When you're in a plane that suddenly goes silent and you see nothing but freezing-cold water below, the only natural reaction is to pray. And fast.

One of those pray-ers that day was Puerto Rican businessman Ric Elias. He lived to tell his story, thanks to some crafty maneuvering from the captain of the flight, who ditched the plane into the river in such a way that every single person survived, all but two without any injury whatsoever. But the crash was still harrowing, and in the minutes it took to actually reach the river, Elias did some deep, if not quick, soul searching. You can learn a lot about people based on how they respond in a crisis, which is why I find his takeaway so interesting: "In that moment," he said, "I regretted the time I was wasted on things that did not matter with people that matter."[6]

There it is: the importance of togetherness. We matter more than stuff ever will.

And yet still, this is the tendency, isn't it? To prioritize the insignificant over the significant, to put people in line after things. We run around like crazed Marthas, forgetting entirely that it was *Mary* whom Jesus praised. We do this, I think, because things can be controlled but people cannot. Things can be accomplished; people are never complete. Things can be kept neat and clean; people are messy every day of their lives. And so we opt for the tidier, more predictable path. To insist on togetherness—at least once a week, anyway—was for us Boyds a way of saying to one another, "Yes, I know you're messy and disheveled and sometimes annoying and quirky and rude, but I'm in. I'm in because I can be all those things, too, and just as desperately, I need people in my life who will love me anyway."

ON BEDHEAD DAYS, GIVE GRACE

And then, a third guideline: *give grace.*

Last week, my assistant, Lex, asked me if I was still working on a book about rest. She'd eyed my calendar on her computer screen mere moments before, which told me it was a loaded question. "I am," I said with a knowing grin, to which she replied, "So your plan is to start living what you're preaching *after* you write the book?"

Laughing, I turned to walk back into my office, but not before saying, "Grace, Lex. Grace."

Despite my best intentions regarding a once-weekly bedhead day, there are weeks when my careful plan doesn't pan out. In those instances, I practice giving myself grace. Rest isn't an obligation; it's a gift—more on this topic in chapter 8. Mark Buchanan wrote:

> The rest of God ... is not a reward for finishing. It's
> not a bonus for work well done.
>> It's sheer gift.[7]

As often as I possibly can, I receive that gift with open arms. But sometimes life presents obstacles that are unavoidable, and the gift sits there, still beautifully wrapped.

A month ago, a massive wildfire overtook our local news coverage and our very lives, and our church was converted to a Red Cross shelter to house displaced residents from area neighborhoods.

I was helping staff the shelter with a team of New Lifers, making sure evacuees had food and bottles of water and warm blankets and sturdy cots, all on the day that was my bedhead day for the week. Still, I knew I was where I needed to be, even as my day of rest was usurped. As I put my head on my pillow that night, I thought about how grateful I was for the progress I'd made over the years, with regard to living a rhythmic life.

This fire was a bona fide emergency, but there was a time in my life when I wouldn't have perceived it as such. Back then I was living as though *all of life* were an emergency and, consequently, never saw real crises for what they were—deviations from the norm, not the norm itself. I was learning, wasn't I? Against all odds, I was becoming something of a Sabbath keeper—not a perfect one, admittedly, but one who practiced, anyway. "Astonishing material and revelation appear in our lives all the time," Anne Lamott once said. "Let it be. Unto us, so much is given. We just have to be open for business."[8]

BREAKING BUSY

Challenge #1: Call Impression Management What It Is

Self-help writers and well-meaning pastors alike proclaim the virtues of living authentic lives, of being ourselves, of letting down our guard, of forgetting about what others think. And while it is true that living in this manner does great things for our minds and hearts, it doesn't change the fact that it's a really difficult way to live! Most of us have carefully architected walls surrounding us that don't get demolished overnight. No, we've established these habits because we feel safe here, inside our intentionally crafted facades. We like managing others' impression of us. We like being our own PR rep. And yet if we were honest, we'd have to admit that keeping up appearances is an exhausting way to live.

On a sheet of paper or in your journal, note the habits you maintain for the sheer sake of impression management. Maybe you insist on yours being the first car in the parking lot at your place of employment. Or on having the latest, most fashion-forward clothes. Or on driving the cleanest, most powerful car. Or on being up-to-date on breaking news every day. If you're a woman, maybe you never leave the house without makeup on—even to run to the grocery store. Be honest with yourself as you log these habits: *What is it I always do, so that others will be impressed by me?*

Challenge #2: Give a Bedhead Day a Try

Next, give a bedhead day a try. If your list of impression-management habits is lengthy, you may short-circuit at the idea of tabling all of them for a full day. But perhaps you can choose one or two of them—getting to work early, for example, instead of coming in on time, or else dressing to the nines just to attend a casual outing with your family—and determine to let them go for a day. Then, throughout the day, take note of how you feel in your spirit when you're not utterly consumed with what others may think.

5

SHABBAT SHALOM

The day [Sabbath] is thick with peace.
—MaryAnn McKibben Dana

REST IS MADE FOR US

I love to travel—always have, and probably always will. I love eating
food items I don't normally eat, seeing sights I don't normally see,
and traipsing about foreign lands. I love seeing how people do life on
the other side of the planet and having my horizons expanded and
enriched as I go.

Here's what's also true: I always love coming home. I love coming home because in my home, everything is "just so." The foods I
like are there, and they are right where I like them to be. The pillow
I like is there, and it is always on "my" side of the bed. The closet in
my bedroom contains the clothes I like to wear. The truck I like to

drive is always right there, in the garage. My home is perfectly suited for me—my patterns, my preferences, my tastes, and my desires. It fits me like a glove. In fact, it was arranged with me in mind.

Interestingly, the Bible says the Sabbath works the same way. "The Sabbath was made to serve us," Jesus told his disciples in Mark 2:27. "We weren't made to serve the Sabbath."

The context of this verse is fantastic. Four verses prior, we learn that Jesus is walking through a field of ripe grain with his disciples. As they carve a path through the tall stalks of wheat, some of the disciples pull off a few heads of grain. They were hungry, and so they ate. But this was on the Sabbath—a fact the Pharisees who were tagging along decided to draw attention to. "Look!" those law keepers said to Jesus. "Your disciples are breaking Sabbath rules!" (v. 24).

The "rules" the Pharisees were referring to included a whole host of parameters the Hebrew people had set forth generations prior. Specifically, they were taking issue with one of the thirty-nine categories of banned activities, known as "reaping"—removing all or part of a plant from its source of growth. This was forbidden on the Sabbath because it was considered work, an activity of creation, and this was to be a day of non-creation, a day of rest.

Which brings us to Jesus's response about the Sabbath being made for us, instead of the other way around. His perspective, essentially, was this: Moses and the prophets may have set forth the schedule of Sabbath, but I—Jesus—have come to establish the spirit of it. And the spirit of it is one of peace, not of prohibition.

An early realization I came to in my bedhead-day observance was that I could be the most scheduled, efficient, dutiful person on the planet and yet if I missed the spirit of the Sabbath, I was missing the glory God intended for it.

In this world, we are promised a little chaos. For some of us, we're promised a lot. "In this godless world you will continue to experience difficulties," Jesus said in John 16:33. "But take heart! I've conquered the world." And interestingly, the way Jesus conquers the world is not by acts of war but by acts of pervasive peace. It is peace that brings us to Christ. It is peace that saves our souls. And it is peace that saves our weeks from peril, the peace of a day of rest. God knew we'd need peace once a week, just as we need our own bed after being on the road for a week. He knew we'd need a soft place to land, a plumb line to recenter our souls. And so, the Sabbath—an invitation, a gift, a small taste on the tongue of peace.

In Jewish tradition, there is a name for this: "Shabbat shalom"— literally, "may your day of no work be peaceful."[1] One person would say this as a greeting to another, and that person would respond in kind: "May your day of no work be peaceful as well."

Because God is not only the inventor of peace but also himself *Peace*, another way of saying it is, "May God be in your rest, and may you be in the rest of God." A day of rest is a day to know peace, to experience and express the peace of God.

DEMANDING TO SIMPLY STOP

I've been in Jerusalem on several occasions, and each time I'm there over a Sabbath, I'm struck by how seriously the Jews take their day of rest. In Jerusalem, you can't get anything done on the Sabbath. Nothing. The whole town essentially shuts down. You might find a store or two open that are owned by Arabs, but I guarantee all Jewish shopkeepers are closed for the day. They're at home or at a synagogue with their families, enjoying a Sabbath meal, enjoying the pleasure of one another's company, and enjoying the inner strength that comes when we rest.

The last time I was in Israel, my traveling companions and I accidentally got into the wrong elevator at our hotel. Unwittingly, we'd boarded the *Shabbat* elevator, the elevator reserved for Sabbath observation, the elevator that won't let you push any buttons but instead stops on every single floor. Pushing buttons would constitute work, and work is not to be done on that day.

It's a little legalistic for my taste, honestly, but I do appreciate the point. The point is this: at some point, *stop*. Stop! Quit running and gunning and pushing all the buttons that control your life and simply choose to rest.

The Hebrew people understood the importance of this type of sacred rest, and the Old Testament is peppered with stories of their devotion to Sabbath rest, even during the most perilous parts of their lives. "They kept Sabbath under siege," wrote Mark Buchanan. "They kept it in famine. They kept it in drought."

Buchanan went on to say, "Their keeping it nurtured something deep and hidden in them that came to light only on the day of testing."[2]

But the Hebrew people were still people, and as such, they were an imperfect lot. They kept the Sabbath faithfully, until they didn't. And when they didn't, God got on their case. It wasn't so much that they had abandoned Sabbath keeping; they hadn't. They had turned it into a day just to get ahead, which kind of defeated the purpose of a day given to us for rest. Isaiah 58 contains one of the strictest warnings and also one of the sweetest promises ever issued to the Israelites by God. Verses 13 and 14 read:

> "If you watch your step on the Sabbath
> and don't use my holy day for personal
> advantage,
> If you treat the Sabbath as a day of joy,
> GOD's holy day as a celebration,
> If you honor it by refusing 'business as usual,'
> making money, running here and there—
> Then you'll be free to enjoy GOD!
> Oh, I'll make you ride high and soar above it
> all.
> I'll make you feast on the inheritance of your
> ancestor Jacob."
> Yes! GOD says so!

Here, God is committing to his people—the Israelites of old, and also us, here, today—that if they, if we, will simply rest, then we will find freedom; we will find enjoyment of God. We will, in short, find peace. It's something we find by no other means. Remember that? It's something we find only by resting in God.

I got a call last week from a church staff member who works at a church positioned only a few miles from where a school shooting occurred. Several of that church's families had kids who were murdered that day, and soon after the tragedy, the senior pastor of the church called to see if I would be willing to walk with them through the grief that had descended on their congregation like an ominous black cloud. I said yes, and for many months now, I have been fielding phone calls and making site visits and praying earnest prayers on behalf of that strong but heartbroken body of believers.

It was the pastor's assistant who was calling now, a gentle woman originally from England who has made her home here in the States for several years. "Pastor Brady," she said in her lilting British accent, "we are all at our wit's end here and simply don't know what to do. We are exhausted."

She sounded tired, even over the phone.

I happened to be on vacation as I took the call, and there in my Florida hotel room, I motioned for Pam and the kids to go on to the beach without me. I flashed five fingers twice, signaling I'd join them in ten minutes or so. And then I made myself comfortable in an oversize chair that overlooked the ocean, and prayed for a string of wise words to say to this woman who clearly was at the end of her rope.

"Tell me about your typical week," I started. "What I'm asking is, despite all that there is to do right now, when do you ever rest?"

If anyone understands the demands on a pastor and his or her staff following a congregational tragedy, I do. There are media demands to accommodate. There are meetings with family members to coordinate and then subsequent follow-up actions to tend to. There are practical needs to meet. Albeit not on par at all with the level of agony for the immediate family members who actually suffered the loss, there's your own grief and despair to somehow work through. The tendency is to keep serving, keep communicating, and keep offering up resources of time and money and love. And while this is a very good, very godly response, it doesn't exactly facilitate periods of rest. My friends suffering at that church dealing with the school shooting know this reality all too well.

In response to my question, the pastor's assistant said, "Well, I have Fridays off. And Saturday mornings."

Her church held services not just on Sunday mornings but also on Saturday nights, which meant that at least a portion of the staff had a heavy load of responsibility each Saturday afternoon, as preparations were made for the evening's service. What she was really saying was, "I work six days a week and use the other day, the seventh day, to tend to my personal life."

"Tell me what you do on an average Friday," I then said.

She replied, "Oh, I get my car washed and pick up groceries. I'll get my hair cut or have my oil changed. You know, the usual errands."

I let the silence following her comment sit there for a moment before I offered up my thoughts. Finally, I said this: "I understand the amount of stress you and your colleagues are under. You know I do. What happened in your community is devastating, and now you and others are left to pick up the broken pieces and try desperately to move on. But I have to tell you the truth here, which is that while those things you mentioned are perfectly good things to do on your one and only day off each week, they are not things that will bring you rest."

Her silence spoke more than words could.

"You've got to carve out time for rest," I continued, which will be a problem for her, I know. During visits with other members of her church's senior leadership team, I picked up on a distinctly workaholic vibe. And when senior leaders don't rest, nobody rests. The bar has been set too high.

There was more silence from her end, but I continued, "You already know everything I am telling you now. You're calling me today because you recognize that the pace you're living by is unsustainable, and because you're looking for a way to slow things down. Am I right?"

Through a knowing sigh, she murmured, "Right."

"The only solution here is rest. You can try a thousand other things—telling yourself this is just a season and things will slow down soon; distracting yourself with busyness and hoping your soul doesn't notice what's up; taking sleeping pills, drinking too much alcohol, overeating, and more—but what I'm telling you is the truth: the only solution is rest. You can't ignore the Sabbath and survive. Take it from a guy who tried. I know you're doing all these good things for God, but these good and godly things are going to undo you in the end."

I could tell what she was thinking, even though she barely spoke another word. She was thinking I didn't understand the demands on her these days—even though she knows full well that I do. She was thinking, *What am I supposed to do, Pastor Brady? Turn into a negligent slacker at work?*

This *is* what we think, isn't it? That if we don't give 100 percent every minute of every day, we are not deserving of our role. We think that if we don't return every email and every phone call right this minute, that if we don't make every meeting, that if we don't respond to every request, that if we don't apply ourselves fully at all points throughout a given day, the universe will utterly fall apart.

Expanding the idea beyond the walls of a church, we think if we don't get every room vacuumed, every bookshelf dusted, every meal made by hand, every child's homework folder initialed, every birthday party attended, every plant watered, every inch of grass mowed, every load of laundry folded, every lacrosse practice made, every book read, every app mastered, every televised sporting event watched, every *everything* done, we will somehow be lesser human beings.

I myself had lived according to that philosophy for far too many years. I'm here to tell you it's bunk. The whole philosophy is bunk. The universe will keep on spinning, and you will keep on being a great person, even if a few things are left undone.

A New Zealand Prayer Book has a fantastic prayer in it called "Night Prayer," and one of the stanzas reads, "It is night after a long day. What has been done has been done; what has not been done has not been done; let it be."[3] Do what you can do and then "let it be." Really. Life will go on. This is what I tell the men and women I oversee at New Life, that if they choose burnout for themselves (because I will certainly not inflict it on them), I *will* come to their funeral and I *will* say nice things about them, but I absolutely *will not* cry. I won't cry because I will know that this is how they wanted to die; they wanted to literally run themselves into the ground.

New Life staffers know full well that I expect them to do their jobs in less than fifty hours a week and that they are not to be away from their homes more than two or three nights a week for the purposes of doing ministry. If they choose to work more hours than what I mandate, then I pull them in for a little chat. One of two things clearly is wrong: they have too much to do and we need to revisit their task load, or else they are not working smart. Either way, something has to change. I know it. They know it. His or her spouse knows it. In fact, a call from a spouse is typically how I discover that a particular staff member is working too many hours. New Life staff spouses know that I expect them to call my cell if their husbands or wives are violating my fifty-hour rule. I've received a few of those phone calls over the years, and you'd better believe I take them to heart. I pull in the staff member, we have a conversation, and together we chart a new course.

During those conversations, I remind them that if they do wish to burn out, there are plenty of churches around this country that will welcome them with open arms. But New Life is not one of them. I help them remember that they are part of a church community that is staunchly antiburnout.

REFUSING TO BE ENSLAVED

God has given us everything we need in order to live rhythmic, well-rested lives. To ignore these divine resources is to sign up for slavery, again and again and again. This is true because rest is freedom; the unrested live unfree. Again from Buchanan:

> To refuse Sabbath is in effect to spurn the gift of
> freedom. It is to resume willingly what we once

cried out for God to deliver us from. It is choosing what we once shunned.

Slaves don't rest. Slaves can't rest. Slaves, by definition, have no freedom to rest. Rest, it turns out, is a condition of liberty....

Sabbath is a refusal to go back to Egypt.[4]

When you enter the rest of God, the peace of God, you declare, "I'm not going back. I'm not going back to the patterns and practices and propensities that made my life chaotic and cold. I'm putting down the spinning plates; I'm climbing down from the ladder; I'm allowing the exhale to emerge." It's entering the future, now.

What does this freedom look like for you, this foretaste of kingdom come? The smell of falling rain? The sound of wind in trees? A morning to sleep in? The ability to lose track of time while reading a book? Making homemade soup? Simply focusing on your breath for a few minutes? Meandering through a list of chores? Listening—really listening—to your spouse or your kids? Talking candidly with God? Leisure time that's leisurely, for once?

My friend Brian Zahnd said that what we must do in order to determine what freedom is for us is to ask ourselves (in that future reality) things such as, "What will be abolished? What will be maintained? What will be restored?" Then, once we are courageous enough to answer those questions, we must work "for the abolition, maintenance, and restoration of these things."[5] Remember, it was for this and all forms of freedom that Christ set us free, says Galatians 5:1. "So take your stand! Never again let anyone put a harness of slavery on you."

In my book *Sons and Daughters*, I tell the story of Abraham Lincoln enacting the Emancipation Proclamation in the mid-eighteen hundreds, thereby freeing every person in this country who was being held as a slave, one forced to work against his or her will. Government officials would go knocking on doors of slave owners, in order to tell the slaves that at last they'd been freed, but rather than those slaves quickly packing up their belongings and rushing away, they actually chose to stay put.

Their grandparents had been slaves. Their parents had been slaves. And they had been slaves most of their lives. Servitude was all they knew, and servitude, for them, was home.

On this issue of rest, you and I have a legacy too. We pass on to our children and grandchildren either a legacy of rhythmic living or else a legacy of chaos and unrest; either we pass on proper abolishment, maintenance, and restoration, or else, tragically, we don't.

Not surprisingly, God prefers we pass on peace, even though we so often don't make that choice.

I was recently talking with a group of parents whose kids are in club sports, and one of the moms present was lamenting how busy her family's life always is. "This is what our weeks are like," she said. "My husband and I work full-time Monday through Friday, while our kids are in school. On Friday afternoon, he and I get off work, we swing by the house to pick up the kids, we pile into the Suburban, and we head clear across the state to a volleyball tournament. Or basketball. Or soccer, depending on the kid and depending on the weekend. We arrive at a motel sometime Friday night, check in, double-check our kid's gear, and get as much rest as is possible when you're sleeping on scratchy sheets in a room with an annoying air conditioner that clicks on and off every five minutes. We get up Saturday, watch either our daughter or one of our sons play sports all day long, get back to the hotel Saturday night, grab some dinner—and I use the term 'dinner' loosely—and collapse on the bed at ten o'clock. We get up Sunday morning and do it all over again. Once our sports obligations are finished, we pile back into the SUV, head home, and arrive dead tired and ready for bed."

She said that all the parents convene in the hotel lobby Sunday morning before they have to leave for day two of the tournament, bemoaning the fact that they are there, again, in some random motel lobby, exhausted and disillusioned that this has become their life. They do this every single weekend, week after week after week.

I took in this woman with bags under her eyes and said, "So let me get this straight. You've decided that the best way to cover college tuition for your kids is to have them get in on a sports scholarship, right? And the only way they can compete for those monies is to be *that good* at sports from a very young age."

She was expressionless, which I took to mean yes.

"On the high end," I continued, "school will run, what, forty grand a year? Let's use that as a rough figure, anyway, which means one hundred and sixty grand when it's all said and done, give or take. You spend five or six grand per year to enroll your kid in club sports, from age eight to eighteen. *Boom.* There's sixty grand. You spend a hundred bucks a night for hotel rooms, times two nights per weekend, times about twenty weekends a year, times a decade. *Boom.* Another forty grand. Factor in food and snacks and top-of-the-line gear and private sessions with skills instructors, and really, you're lucky if it doesn't cost you *more* than the one-sixty in the end. Am I right?"

More blank expressions from the mom. And then this: "Well, you can't put a price on keeping kids out of trouble these days. When they're busy, they don't have sex. When they're busy, they don't do drugs. When they're busy, they don't hang out with the wrong crowd—for me, that price is the one I don't want to pay."

It was a good-natured conversation. Really, it was. Which is why it was so easy for me to then add, "Maybe so. But you're compromising your kids' childhoods in the end. This isn't simple math. This isn't a break-even thing. It's a loss. All the way around, it's a loss. Your kids are going to be worn out. *You* are going to be worn out. And all of you will go through the rest of your lives never knowing how to relish rest."

We want the "blessings" of being a peacemaker Jesus speaks of in the Sermon on the Mount, even as we brazenly choose not to live at peace.

In one sense, I was the pot calling the kettle black here, and I told her so. I've fought my share of rest-versus-restlessness battles along the way, and my heart was to share what I had learned. Her response was a helpless shrug of the shoulders, with hands upturned in the air.

DEALING SPARINGLY IN THIS LIFE

Practically speaking, my observation is that when kids are never taught how to appreciate healthy rhythms, once they escape the frenetic pace their parents have maintained on their behalf, they rebel as though Rebellion is their middle name. Busyness has become their business, and when that busyness disappears, they don't know what to do with their lives. They don't know what to do with an idle thought, let alone an idle day. To this point Tim Kreider, writer of "The 'Busy' Trap" article, said: "Idleness is not just a vacation, an indulgence or a vice; it is as indispensable to the brain as vitamin D is to the body, and deprived of it we suffer a mental affliction as disfiguring as rickets."[6] Most people who suffer from rickets are kids, and most kids who get it are starving. I realize that in twenty-first-century North America, a majority of kids are not starving from food, but I guarantee they are starving for *something*—for calmness, for quietness, for rest.

Our kids were young when Pam and I decided to unplug one day a week. and it was a countercultural move, to be sure. In Southlake, the Land of People with Means, parents enroll their kids in everything under the sun, and as a result, they never have a day off. Unlike nearly every other toddler we knew, Abram and Callie were not in gymnastics classes, dance classes, horseback-riding classes, foreign-language classes, art classes, etiquette classes, or classes that taught tae kwon do. As three- and five-year-olds, they were not on soccer teams, basketball teams, debate teams, cheerleading squads, or in science clubs, and those tiny fingers never played piano once. Sure, various activities would emerge as they got older—including basketball and tae kwon do. But in those early years, even in the face of mounting pressure, we chose to simply stay home.

In 1 Corinthians 7:29–31, the apostle Paul wrote, "I do want to point out, friends, that time is of the essence. There is no time to waste, so don't complicate your lives unnecessarily. Keep it simple—in marriage, grief, joy, whatever. Even in ordinary things—your daily routines of shopping, and so on. Deal as sparingly as possible with the things the world thrusts on you. This world as you see it is on its way out."

Keep it simple. Uncomplicated. Dealing as sparingly as possible. *Huh?* Is this really possible, Paul?

Pam and I decided it was. And we ordered our lives according to that truth. We let the hyperscheduled families zoom right past us, while we stayed hunkered down inside our peaceful home. And you know what? We were better for it. We recognized how well our kids did when we didn't have plans for them on those days. We saw that if we gave our kids time and space to breathe, to exhale, to just be kids, they flourished. From time to time, we wondered if they were missing out on something—if by not learning an instrument or a foreign language at age three, they'd somehow suffer later on. But by the end of each bedhead day, we'd have our answer again. A day of rest was pure benefit for them. "Just as our children depend on us for three meals a day," wrote Katrina Kenison, "they also need us to prepare peaceful spaces for them in the midst of this busy world."[7] There was nothing for Abram and Callie but upside, by our choosing not to run ragged, by choosing to live joyfully at rest.

LIVING THE SHEMA

Still today, I notice that my best conversations with my kids—and in Callie's case, the only conversations, really—occur either right when they get up in the morning or right before they go to bed, during typical periods of rest.

Abram is always the first one up at our house. After I woke this morning, I made my way to the kitchen in search of a cup of hot coffee, and there sat Abram—still groggy and with sleep in his eyes. Pam and Callie were still sleeping, which is generally the case around the Boyd household, and as I waited for my coffee to brew, I asked Abram how he slept. It was a benign question, really—I was just filling the silence until my cup was full. But it turns out that he slept great and that he had this amazing series of dreams he was all too eager to tell me about. One of the dreams featured a new invention he has been thinking about, and that it was really true, he was sure, just as we've talked about for years and years, that one day he would create something that would absolutely change the world.

Abram's body may have still been weary, but his brain was crystal clear. This came as no surprise to me. Abram's brain is always clear at six o'clock in the morning.

My daughter, Callie, is her brother's polar opposite. She is virtually mute until noon and even then keeps her cards close to the vest. But check back in with her before bedtime and you'll have a veritable chatterbox on your hands. At the close of the day, Callie's thoughts are lucid; she finally calms down enough to look you straight in the eye and string together sentences that let you in.

It's no coincidence that my kids come alive early in the morning and late at night; God predicted this would be true. In Jewish tradition, the centerpiece of morning and evening prayer services is a passage of Scripture known as the Shema, from Deuteronomy 6:4–9. It reads:

> Hear, O Israel: The LORD our God, the LORD is one.
> Love the LORD your God with all your heart and

with all your soul and with all your strength. These commandments that I give you today are to be on your hearts. Impress them on your children. Talk about them when you sit at home and when you walk along the road, when you lie down and when you get up. Tie them as symbols on your hands and bind them on your foreheads. Write them on the doorframes of your houses and on your gates. (NIV)

I loved this passage even before I became a parent, and even more so after Abram and Callie were ours. There is such insight here! God says, in effect, "Love me, and then teach your kids to love me. Enjoy me, and then teach your kids to do the same." This is what we do when we become people of peace. We reside in the rest of God, and our kids learn to reside there too. And we do this, says the Shema, by using our downtime to instruct them in truth. We are to talk about the Word of God, the truth of God, when we're hanging out at home and when we're traveling across town and when we climb into bed at night and when we get up the very next day. You'll notice that this Old Testament passage assumes we actually have downtime to fill. It assumes that we're actually talking with our kids each day.

Personal experience has taught me that if I don't carve out time for relaxed conversations with my kids (hello, hot tub!), they will take the pressing questions all kids have banging around in their brains to someone else. All the curiosities that come with adolescence—*Who is God? What am I here for? What is sin? Why does it matter? What is success? What do I do with failure? Does anybody really see me or care?*—don't cease to exist because we as parents are too preoccupied, too busy to answer them. No, the questions persist. We just won't be there when they're finally asked. If we are always at the office and always exhausted when we get home, our kids will stuff their questions until they can't stuff them anymore. And then the next time they're over at a friend's house, they'll ask that pimply teenager their pressing questions instead. Similarly, if our kid is always at lacrosse practice and barely has time to breathe outside of that, then guess who is going to be answering that child's pressing questions? The lacrosse coach, probably. Or else a teammate's mom, the one who always gives your kid a ride home.

God placed our kids in our specific families with the expectation that *we* will train them in righteousness and truth. We are responsible for teaching them how to think critically, how to behave morally, how to put their faith and trust in a loving God. But we can't do these things if we aren't living these things first. In one author's words, "If you want your teenager [or preteen, or toddler, for that matter] to have an understanding of Sabbath … and to understand time as more than a container for text messages and soccer tournaments and term papers, then start with yourself."[8] It really is true: we can't give away what we ourselves don't have.

BREAKING BUSY

Challenge #1: Let It Be

Tonight, as you prepare for bed, say aloud those words from *A New Zealand Prayer Book*: "What has been done has been done; what has not been done has not been done; let it be." Speak the sentiment over your day—regardless of what the day held or did not hold, and exhale your desire for the day to have looked differently. Accept it for what it was—and also for what it wasn't—and rest easy tonight.

Challenge #2: Select a Day to Stop

Whether for your first time or your ten thousandth, select a day to simply stop. Stop your business dealings, stop your running around town, and stop your incessant desire to check your Twitter feed. *Stop.* Eyeball your calendar, and choose a day this week or next when you will not merely take a day off, but when you will actually *rest*. Write *SABBATH* in all caps on that day, and then commit to protecting it at all costs. Sort out child care, give family members and colleagues a heads-up, tackle chores and obligations beforehand, and then let the peace of God invade your life for a complete day. Sit. Read. Reflect. Journal. Do whatever you are led to do, as long as it invites you to stop and rest.

6

THE JESUS PACE

Imagine all the people living life in peace.
—John Lennon

WHAT JESUS KNEW THAT I DON'T

The truth about me is that despite brief periods of impressive wholeness and holiness as it relates to living a rhythmic life, I'm still and likely always will be a hyperscheduled person, a sign-me-up slave to the clock. Left to my own less-than-stellar devices, I become irritable when there is no schedule to speak of and even more irritable when there is a schedule to speak of and somebody has the gall to disrupt it. This doesn't bode well for someone seeking to live the Jesus pace; you don't exactly see him consulting his daily agenda on his smartphone every sixty seconds. At times I think I'm getting better, that I'm learning to take some things in stride. But in the same way that an addict is always an addict, I recognize that as it relates to time, I'll always be counting my sober days.

My problem stems from a little something Jesus said about what it means to be in relationship with him. Just this morning I was rereading the piece about how he says that the people who want to be his disciples will do some very strange things, such as *denying themselves* and *taking up their crosses daily* and *following him.*[1]

I can barely clear the first bar: Deny myself? Seriously? Why would I want to do that? I *like* myself. I like what my self wants, what it needs … and what it so often wants and needs is control. Or the illusion of control, at least.

I have a seat at my desk. I exhale and notice that the simple process of breathing puts a tiny bit of wind in my sails. I think about that verse in Romans, where the apostle Paul says that he does what he doesn't want to do and doesn't do what he knows he should. I don't really want to be thinking about it, because I know it will not absolve but indict me. But think about it, I do. Specifically, I think about Eugene Peterson's rendering, which says that one of the most perplexing things about ourselves is that we decide one way, but then act another. Oh, how I can relate.

The fuller passage in Romans 7 reads:

> What I don't understand about myself is that I decide one way, but then I act another, doing things I absolutely despise. So if I can't be trusted to figure out what is best for myself and then do it, it becomes obvious that God's command is necessary. But I need something *more*! For if I know the

law but still can't keep it, and if the power of sin within me keeps sabotaging my best intentions, I obviously need help …. It happens so regularly that it's predictable. The moment I decide to do good, sin is there to trip me up. I truly delight in God's commands, but it's pretty obvious that not all of me joins in that delight. Parts of me covertly rebel, and just when I least expect it, they take charge. I've tried everything and nothing helps. I'm at the end of my rope. Is there no one who can do anything for me? Isn't that the real question? (vv. 15–17, 21–24)

The command—the "law"—I'm butting up against here lately is the one about rest. The Sabbath wasn't a suggestion; originally it was a law. And before that, it was a practice that God himself kept. Creation: six days. Rest: day seven. Clearly he didn't need rest; he is God, after all. No, he was modeling something here, something I am supposed to tune in to.

And yet my mind spins out of control—literally—when something interrupts my plan. I'm living too close to the margins again, which means every interruption is a step closer to boundarylessness. I don't think this is what God had in mind.

The apostle Paul had a solution, one I'm planning to cling to as well. According to him, it turns out there *is* someone who can do something for him—no surprise, it's Jesus Christ. Verse 25 speaks of this: "He acted to set things right in this life of contradictions where I want to serve God with all my heart and mind [e.g., give a rip about any agenda but my own, when I am informed that someone besides me has a need], but am pulled by the influence of sin to do something totally different."

So, Jesus.

It always comes back to Jesus.

Wonderfully and annoyingly, it always comes back to him.

I think about his ways, about his pace. About Lazarus and how Lazarus had died and how Jesus was told that Lazarus had died and how that news totally rerouted Jesus and yet, somehow, he didn't mind. Admittedly, he didn't rush to get there, but when did Jesus ever rush? When he did arrive, he ministered to Lazarus's sisters, wept his own bitter tears over the loss, and then—wow—even raised the dead. He was so life giving in his response that he literally resuscitated the one who had died.

The contrast is striking. I don't exactly respond to interruptions this way.

I stay planted there in my desk chair and take some time to excavate the "Jesus pace." There's a lot for me to learn, me of the devoted bedhead-day practice, me, the one who still so often balks at the rhythmic life.

THE JESUS PACE IS RHYTHMIC

A string of scenes from Luke 5 catches my attention first. Here Jesus is, right in the thick of ministry, calling disciples to follow him; enfolding sinners in community; and healing people who are paralyzed and marginalized, broken and bruised and sad. He is teaching and preaching and answering questions about the kingdom until his voice is hoarse. He's working hard and pushing hard and running fast and strong. But in the midst of all this busyness, Jesus decides to take a break. In fact, he takes many well-deserved breaks. "As often as possible," Luke 5:16 says, "Jesus withdrew to out-of-the-way places for prayer."

He withdraws in order to work through tragic news, such as when he learns that his friend John the Baptist has died.[2] He withdraws to gain insight on important decisions, such as which men to call to follow him.[3] He withdraws so that he simply can pray.[4] He withdraws to enjoy time with his closest companions.[5] He withdraws as a means of teaching his disciples the unparalleled value of rest.[6] He doesn't wait until his mission is accomplished. He doesn't wait until someone sanctions a few days off for him. He doesn't even wait for an official "Sabbath" to dawn. When he senses it's time to withdraw, he just goes.

"Jesus obeyed a deeper rhythm,"[7] wrote Wayne Muller. Absolutely, he does just that: engage, engage, engage, *withdraw* … engage, engage, engage, *withdraw*.

Rhythmic—that's how Jesus lived.

It's how we're invited to live too.

We're invited to work hard and retreat frequently and trust that whatever falls through the cracks while we're retreating will get tackled during our next working-hard time. The universe really will keep spinning, as I've promised you. Even in our absence, it goes around.

I myself am not entirely convinced this is true, you understand. You'd pick up on this if you observed me for a few days. But credible people I know say it is so, including Senator Joe Lieberman, a guy pegged as unlikely to write a book on sacred rest. And yet he did. In it, he wrote, "None of us needs to work every day of the week. A lot of people think they are perpetually indispensable—to their families, to their co-workers, to themselves, maybe even to the world. If I don't go to work, my career will be ruined. If I don't go shopping, my family will starve. If I don't go to the gym, my body will atrophy."[8]

There's that ugly fear again, that if we don't keep all the plates spinning, they might just crash to the floor. And, oh, the mess that would make. Secretly we're afraid that if we don't keep doing what we've always done, all of life will fall apart. That woman at the church near the school shooting isn't the only one. We all think this is true.

In our better, brighter moments, we see that of course this is not the case. We see that we are not the sum of our spinning plates. We see that we desperately need to rest.

When we finally do withdraw, we can take courage from the fact that Jesus saw fit to withdraw too. Following suit, we, too, can leave the prevailing busyness that tends to run our lives; we can leave the "people with needs" who threaten to implode if we really do go; we can leave the stuff of preoccupation in favor of the peace we so desperately seek. We can do all these things because Jesus did them and because he was showing us how to live. Poets say he withdrew to be reminded of his heavenly home. I say he did it to show us what a rhythmic life is like, to show us that divine rest is not an obligation but an invitation. And to show us what it's like to respond with a heartfelt yes.

This is where I'd missed the point, just as the Jews in Jesus's day missed the point. I'd started institutionalizing my rest, insisting that it had to start at a certain time on a certain day, each and every week, and that when something or someone got in the way of it, that diversion would equal my doom. My rest had become my lord, something I had to appease, lest I died. Jesus never saw rest this way. Remember his declaration in Mark 2:27? "The Sabbath was made for man," he said to his disciples, "not man for the Sabbath" (NIV).

To the Jewish people listening that day, shock must have registered in their hearts. They had spent their entire lives orienting themselves around the rules and regulations of Sabbath observation. What on earth did Jesus mean?

He wasn't trying to be disrespectful; he was declaring truth. They'd totally missed the point by turning God's rest into a list of to-dos. D. A. Carson wrote:

> The giving of the Sabbath law was not meant to be a burden; in fact the Sabbath was to reflect God's compassion for His people, as well as to emphasize the character of His holiness. But this intention was forgotten in arrogance and rebellion as legalism and traditionalism grew. The true concept of the Sabbath law was proclaimed again and again by God's prophets who stressed the covenant relationship, but people were unwilling to listen. Instead of understanding it to be their privilege to rest on Sabbath, they viewed it as deprivation; instead of recognizing their opportunity to commune with God, they saw only inconvenience and hardship. Rather than discovering freedom to worship, they felt in bondage to a law, and instead of grasping the idea of renewal of their covenant relationship to God, they experienced the tragedy of legalism.[9]

Jesus wasn't into legalism, evidenced in the way he "worked" on various Sabbaths—picking wheat, healing disfigured people—and also in the way he rested when people thought he should work. What has always been most notable about Jesus's voluntary withdrawals is not that he rested but when he chose to rest. He withdrew to rest when people still needed him and also when his ego would have been tempted to stay. Jesus didn't merely rest when rest was expected; he also rested when he was at the top of his game.

THE JESUS PACE IS RELATIONAL

To that issue of differentiating when it's time to engage and when it's time to withdraw, I notice that Jesus did another thing really well: he listened to the voice of his Father, and he let those divine whispers guide his life.

This, of course, is what all that "withdrawing" was about. It was about carving out time to pray, to commune, and to lean in.

I was trying to explain this idea recently to a good friend and said, "It's like this: What if Pam and I invited you and your husband over for dinner, and then, as soon as you arrived, she and I jumped into the car and headed out to run a few errands? You're left standing there on our front porch, holding the hospitable bouquet of flowers you brought, wondering why you got ditched by your dinner hosts."

You and I would be flabbergasted by that turn of events too, wouldn't we? If you get invited to someone's home for dinner, you kind of expect that someone to be there. You expect to have quality time with him or her, you expect to enjoy unhurried conversation, you expect for things being centered on the get-together at hand.

This is exactly how Jesus treated God. His times of withdrawal, of divine rest, weren't patronizing scraps tossed God's way; they were intentional and intimate moments of connection, during which nothing else caught Jesus's eye. "What you are in love with, what seizes your imagination, will affect everything," Pedro Arrupe said. "It will decide what will get you out of bed in the morning, what you will do with your evening, how you spend your weekends, what you read, whom you know, what breaks your heart, and what amazes you with joy and gratitude. Fall in love, stay in love, and it will decide everything."[10]

Jesus was in love with his Father. And that one great love drove everything he did—and did not do.

It occurred to me as I sat there at my desk this morning that if I had been consumed not with my own plans but instead with entering the rest of God, I would have had reserves from which to joyfully serve those who tend to interrupt my plans. I wouldn't feel so put out inside. For the entirety of Jesus's public ministry here on earth, he was inundated with people every day. And yet not once do I see him exasperated with the humanness of humankind. Yeah, he puts the Pharisees in their place a few times and tells the money changers at the temple to get a life. But I mean regular, everyday people—the people who so often ride my last good nerve. Jesus never seems to be "fed up" with them. He never loses his cool. There is something instructive to me about this, something that looks a lot like being able to engage with people because adequate time has been taken first to engage wholeheartedly with God.

It's been several weeks since I received the phone call—the one from my friend Dan.[11] His marriage had been on the rocks, which I knew; things were now headed for divorce, which I did not. In addition,

Dan said, I should know that he had to enter treatment for alcohol addiction. My mind reeled. This guy is an accomplished professional; a husband, father, and grandfather; someone with enough money in the bank to be financially free the rest of his life … and yet the walls have come tumbling down.

"She's leaving, Brady," he explained, "and she's taking my kids and my money with her." This makes two divorces for Dan, plus myriad relational disasters on the kid and grandkid front. He tells me that he has to sell his five-thousand-square-foot home and soon will be relocating to a tight two-bedroom apartment.

He sums up his years-long condition succinctly: "Clearly, I have issues."

Thankfully, in this moment, I exhibit maturity, growth. "I know you're not really 'into' church," I say, "but come to church this week-end. Come, and sit with me."

Even as the words come out of my mouth, I think back on a conversation Dan and I had one time about church. "Church is whatever I need it to be," he had said, not completely defiantly. I had responded, rather emotionlessly, "That is poor ecclesiology."

I told him that while I agree a church doesn't have to have a big building—or any building, for that matter—the congregation has to be together. Congregations are formed by God for specific purposes, and to neglect the meeting together, both with people you love and admire, and also with people who drive you nuts, is to neglect the greater vision of God. "The sick need to be around the healthy," I had explained that day, "and the healthy need to be around the sick."

I meant vehemently what I had said. Jesus was with Pharisees and prostitutes alike, and left to our own devices, very few of us choose to associate with both ends of a spectrum like that. "Take your hike on Sunday morning. Gather with a few friends over dinner once a week. Meet to pray over a pressing issue," I'd told Dan. "Just don't let those things solely define 'church' for you. Church is the called-out ones. *All* of us, with lives that are messy and neat, alike."

Dan hedges now in response to my offer of church. "I don't know," he says. "I've got to get this apartment thing squared away ..."

This is where we always go, isn't it? To the practical needs of life. We are textbook cases for Abraham Maslow, dutifully climbing his famed pyramid. We focus on food and water before we focus on safety; we focus on safety before we focus on friendship; we focus on friendship before we focus on self-confidence; we focus on self-confidence before we find even a hint of brain space to be moral, spontaneous, and creative. Introduce the search for Jesus into the pyramid, and that's yet another few levels north.

Certainly it is a noble thing, this current societal push, to get everyone clothed and fed and hydrated and sheltered all around our globe. But Jesus says, don't worry first about what you'll eat and wear; worry first about intimacy with me.

Did Maslow have it all wrong?

At least on the phone with my buddy Dan, it seemed obvious to me that in order for him to solve his "issues," as he referred to them, he would need to address not his needs for food and water and a new apartment or safety or friendship or self-confidence or even morality, as good as that is. What he needed was intimacy with his heavenly Father, because everything else flows from that.

Therefore, I had asked him to come to church. I knew that if Dan could encounter the living God, he could gain needed perspective on the rest of his life. Yes, sorting out his housing was important, but it wasn't the most important thing. Yes, making sure he had food to eat was important, but it wasn't the most important thing. Yes, securing his safety by going to an addictions counselor was important, but it wasn't the most important thing.

The most important thing, according to the rhythms of Jesus, was carving out time for God. But really, what time-pressed professional wants to do that? Dan had spent decades lauding efficiency, mandating quick fixes, expecting expediency from all of life. And yet now he faced a dilemma that couldn't be quick-fixed or git-'er-done healed.

Intimacy happens in private, something Jesus knew all too well. This is why he'd scurry away from the crowds and seek out a mountainside where he could be alone. Resting in God is like a series of date nights with your spouse, during which logistics is not the only topic discussed.

"When was the last time you had an intimate moment with God?" I asked Dan before we ended our call.

He quietly exhaled, collected his thoughts, and said without fanfare, "See you Sunday at church."

Dan did come to church. He sat right beside me, there on the front row, and he sang the songs and bowed his head during the prayers and allowed me to place my hands on his shoulders after the service and ask God for his peace to utterly invade Dan's life. Although he would call himself a Christian, Dan would also readily admit that he's never really "walked with Christ." He's never leaned into the peace of his Father and allowed his Father's voice to determine his steps.

I'd never wish devastating circumstances on anyone, but as I watch Dan navigate this season of his life, I can't help but wonder if God is allowing the pain so that something beautiful can be born, something that sniffs of long-awaited, desperately needed peace.

THE JESUS PACE IS RESOLUTE

You could make a case that I have no business pursuing the third part of Jesus's pace until I pass the test on parts one and two. But because I'm a glutton for punishment, I stay at my desk, continue to excavate his lifestyle, and keep on jotting down lessons I've yet to learn. Here's the final one I make a note of: *There's resoluteness to his rest.*

I'm reading in the book of Mark, chapter 4. After a full day of teaching, Jesus, along with his disciples, is on a boat crossing the Sea of Galilee toward the eastern shore. Evidently, without warning, a huge storm erupts, causing waves to pour into the boat and causing the disciples to think they will sink. This happens to make sense to me: if I was on a flight that was going down, I would pray, and if I was on a boat that started to pitch and roll, I would start planning my own funeral too.

So, the storm is surging all around, the disciples are scared out of their minds, and there is Jesus, asleep in the stern. His otherwise happy followers are infuriated. "Is it nothing to you that we're going down?" (v. 38) they scream as Jesus snoozes away.

Finally, he wakes up and surmises the situation and, without any pomp and circumstance, shouts, "Quiet! Settle down!" (v. 39).

He was talking not to the disciples but, astonishingly, to the wind and the waves. More astonishing still: *the wind and the waves complied.*

Mark 4:39 says, "The wind ran out of breath; the sea became smooth as glass."

Wow.

Such confidence. Such resoluteness. Such an awareness of "kingdom come."

But Jesus is simply stunned by the disciples' lack of faith. "Why are you such cowards?" (v. 40) he asks, taking in the wide-eyed and white-knuckled bunch.

The disciples now stagger around not from seasickness, but from sheer awe in the face of this man. "Who is this, anyway?" they ask, according to verse 41. "Wind and sea at his beck and call!"

Try, *all of creation* at his beck and call.

Here's the thing we tend to miss: When Jesus declared peace and quiet, he wasn't declaring it over a single storm; he was declaring it over an entire kingdom. He was saying, in effect, "Peace and quiet will one day reign—everywhere, at all times. At some point, the lion will lie down with the lamb; predator and prey will live at peace."

Interestingly, the Bible never says that the storm that day was caused by Satan. Most likely, it was a naturally occurring storm. Still today, sudden storms can rise up over the mountains of that very region and quickly throw into massive turbulence the otherwise mild Sea of Galilee. This wasn't Satan trying to kill them, then; this was the natural order of things. And what Jesus was saying is that, yes, this is normal and natural for now, but a new normal is on its way in. When my kingdom settles in, all things will be at rest.

What's more, by accusing the disciples of being cowards, he was indicating to them that an unyielding, unwavering confidence could be theirs instead—that they could enjoy that state of rest whenever they chose. This is something they didn't know, and something we have a hard time believing still today. Peace is ours for the taking! It's always knocking on the door; we simply have to open the door and invite it in. We have to be open for business, remember? This is such a fantastic goal. I was starting to understand why Jesus chose to live the way he did. Pace matters. The right pace matters. Perhaps there is hope for me yet.

BREAKING BUSY

Challenge: Practice the Jesus Pace

- *The Jesus Pace Is Rhythmic.* Take a look at your schedule for tomorrow, keeping in mind Jesus's propensity to engage, engage, engage, and then withdraw. In the course of tomorrow's plans, where will you withdraw and allow yourself to rest? Go ahead and block the time or times now, so that you're sure to honor them when they show up. Maybe you have fifteen minutes alone during your morning commute or en route to collect a child from school. Maybe you typically have an hour in the afternoons, when your children are napping. Maybe you have the ability to hole away in your office at work for ten minutes, at the beginning or end of a lunch break. Decide now when you will withdraw, and then tomorrow, commit to doing just that.
- *The Jesus Pace Is Relational.* Specific quiet times alone with God are great, but even greater is a constant flow of communication over the course of a given

day. Just for tomorrow, see if you can't raise your awareness of his presence and his power, and then chat with him as you go about your day. Tell him what's on your heart as you walk from one meeting into the next. Ask him for discernment as you engage in conversation with a friend or associate. Invite God to correct any errant thinking of yours as you reflect on that performance review with your boss. Thank him for the blessings you enjoy in life—your spouse, your kids, your job. Practice chatting with God all throughout the day, and see if the interactions don't work wonders for your spirit by the time you lay your head down that night.

- *The Jesus Pace Is Resolute.* As you walk through tomorrow's agenda, insist on choosing peace. When your toddler is throwing a tantrum, take a deep breath and simply choose peace. When your boss is demanding an impossible deadline, simply choose peace. When there is traffic and construction and the guy behind you is laying on his horn, choose peace. When the annoying family member calls or the needy friend texts, take a step back from the situation and determine in your heart to choose peace. Say the words aloud if that helps you: "I. Choose. Peace." But whatever you do, make peace your choice.

7

CHOOSING MY VINE

I'm afraid of losing my obscurity. Genuineness
only thrives in the dark. Like celery.

—Aldous Huxley

LET'S TALK ABOUT ME

Ten minutes into the requested breakfast meeting, I regretted having said yes. The young man who had asked for the get-together—he needed some pastoral coaching, evidently—was sitting across from me at the diner, and now, there at the restaurant, with my full attention pointed his way, he had the gall to check his smartphone what seemed like every sixteen seconds. He checked it while I was ordering my meal, he checked it just after he ordered his meal, he checked it while I answered his questions, and he even checked it while he asked them. Unless the guy was waiting on word of an organ transplant—which I quickly learned he wasn't—his lack of focus was totally unacceptable. My irritation quickly birthed a fury that made me cut the meeting short, and I bolted.

The world of psychology has a term for this annoying phenomenon of neglecting to pay attention to the person or situation immediately in front of you, choosing instead to see who else is doing something interesting or what else is going on. "FOMO," it is called, otherwise known as the *fear of missing out*. FOMO is what causes us to "text while driving … interrupt one call to take another … check [our] Twitter stream while on a date [or at a breakfast meeting with our pastor!]." In short, we do these infuriating things because "something more interesting or entertaining just *might* be happening."[1] I'm convinced that some of us could experience a visit from Jesus himself—live and in the flesh—and yet still we'd brazenly stick an index finger in the air and say, "Hang on, Jesus. Let me check my Facebook wall real quick."

There is an underlying fear motivating all this craziness—we don't just want to be "in" on other people's excitement; we want them to find us exciting too. We want to be seen and heard and recognized and admired; we so desperately want someone to care. But what's interesting is that when we shout along with hundreds of millions of others who are shouting, still we cannot be heard; our voices are simply lost in the others' me-focused cacophony of sound.

MISSING OUT ON CHRIST

After having considered the pace Jesus lived by, I arrive at an early conclusion: Jesus didn't know FOMO very well. Actually, I don't think he knew it at all. What concerned him was not being included on all the right lists, being retweeted by all the right handles, being known by all the right names. What concerned him was being hidden away in the character of his Father, and from there living life at peace.

John 15 contains a fascinating and interesting metaphor along these lines. Jesus was talking to his disciples and explained his relationship to them in agricultural terms. "I am the Real Vine and my Father is the Farmer," he said. "He cuts off every branch of me that doesn't bear grapes. And every branch that is grape-bearing he prunes back so it will bear even more. You are already pruned back by the message I have spoken" (vv. 1–3).

He then went on to say exactly how this fruit bearing was going to occur: "Live in me. Make your home in me just as I do in you. In the same way that a branch can't bear grapes by itself but only by being joined to the vine, you can't bear fruit unless you are joined with me" (v. 4).

So, it's not that we are expected to live the Jesus pace alone; *he* is the one who will get us there. He is the bandleader in our quest for rhythmic lives.

"I am the Vine," the passage continues. "You are the branches. When you're joined with me and I with you, the relation intimate and organic, the harvest is sure to be abundant. Separated, you can't produce a thing. Anyone who separates from me is deadwood, gathered up and thrown on the bonfire. But if you make yourselves at home with me and my words are at home in you, you can be sure that whatever you ask will be listened to and acted upon. This is how my Father shows who he is—when you produce grapes, when you mature as my disciples" (vv. 5–8).

As it relates to our present-day plague of FOMO, here is what I think Jesus is saying in these verses from John 15: "You're only missing out if you're missing out on me."

OBSCURITY AND WHY WE ABHOR IT

The Bible tells us that just after Jesus was installed in public ministry, he was sent to the back side of the desert by God. Matthew 3:13–17 tells the story of John the Baptist baptizing people in the Jordan River, when Jesus shows up. "He wanted John to baptize him," the text says. "John objected, 'I'm the one who needs to be baptized, not *you*!'

"But Jesus insisted. 'Do it. God's work, putting things right all these centuries, is coming together right now in this baptism.' So John did it.

"The moment Jesus came up out of the baptismal waters, the skies opened up and he saw God's Spirit—it looked like a dove—descending and landing on him. And along with the Spirit, a voice: 'This is my Son, chosen and marked by my love, delight of my life.'"

This was a monumental deal. God is finally raising up his Son as the Messiah; the long-awaited One; the Pretty Big Deal, if ever there was one. Everyone watching that day surely understood the significance of this event. And yet instead of then launching a website, rallying donors, hiring staff, buying a building, or feeding a public-relations frenzy, Jesus simply hid away awhile.

This seems counterproductive, doesn't it? Shouldn't he have—I don't know—made a bigger *splash*?

Evidently, the answer was no. Per his Father's instruction, Jesus willingly left for a forty-day trek in the desert. I've actually been to the part of the world where Bible scholars believe Jesus went during that time, and it is so desolate that it makes the sand dunes of western New Mexico look like a lavish, lush Hawaiian island. It was barren, with a capital *B*.

So, it wasn't just that Jesus withdrew, or even when he withdrew, but also where he withdrew to. He schools us at every turn.

For Jesus, though, this was nothing new. Granted, Jesus's birth was widely publicized, and we do know from Scripture that around age twelve, he was left behind at the temple long after his parents' caravan began the long trip home. But for the most part, the first thirty years of our Savior's life were lived in obscurity. Author Constance Rhodes reminds us:

> Jesus is the great I AM. He is not the great I DO or the great I WILL. His life began with an almost total silence that lasted for thirty years. And then when He finally began His public ministry, many people were disappointed that He didn't do bigger, more far-reaching things. They expected Him to become the king of Israel, to set everything right, everywhere. Instead, He healed sporadically and taught about how to live everyday life.
>
> There were no big Jesus-Heals-'Em-All conventions. While He did the occasional large-scale miracle (such as feeding the five thousand and healing all the sick in a village), for the most part, it was a crippled guy here, a bleeding woman there, a demoniac at the edge of town. And then, strangely, Jesus asked many

of these people to keep it to themselves, not to let the word get out that He had healed them. His disciples must have wondered why a guy with so much power didn't do more with it.[2]

In short, Jesus was at home not being seen.

The Bible frequently uses a device called typology, in which various people, events, institutions, ceremonies, or other things are used to illustrate some truth; one thing is used as a type and shadow of something else. In the Old Testament, for example, both the prophet Moses and King David are intended to be types and shadows of Christ. Not surprisingly, before both men are raised up as the great leaders God has asked them to be, they are found on the back side of the desert, making their home in obscurity.

Frankly, this is information we don't really want to know. We don't care all that much about the stagehands who scurry around in the shadows, dressed in black so they won't be seen, or about the backup singers to the main act. If there's a reason we prize our social-media structures, it's because they allow us to be seen, to be heard, and to be adored. This is what we're after, isn't it? We want to know not how the hidden have stayed hidden but rather how the star rose, how the winner won, how the hero saved the day. "We are deeply conditioned to choose the heroic over the saintly," wrote Brian Zahnd. "We love our heroes best of all."

He goes on: "Heroes are goal-oriented people of great capabilities who know how to make things happen. We admire their ability to get things done and shape the world according to their will. Saints on the other hand—especially to the American mind—seem quaint and marginal, occupying religious spheres on the periphery of the action. We want to be heroes; we don't really want to be saints. The difference between the heroic vision and the saintly vision is a fundamentally different way of viewing the purpose of life."[3]

We want to conquer the world and have everybody know about it. We don't want to be obscure. You and I both have a little group of people where we fit in, where we belong, where we tend to know the score, where we are, in our minds at least, a Pretty Big Deal. To be ostracized and hidden away, to feel like we're missing out on something, is a real challenge, regardless of who we are.

And yet it is here—in obscurity—where we're actually most likely to thrive.

Jan Johnson said, "We were built for times of hard work and outward expression … but also quiet hiddenness…. We must have them both. Crops grow better with a Sabbath; animals labor better with a Sabbath. To pause and know that God is God is wisdom."[4] And so we find that in order to live our lives rhythmically, in order to be Sabbath-keeping, bedhead-day–observing kinds of people, we have to periodically hide ourselves away.

Back to John 15. Each time I read this passage, I feel as though Jesus is holding up a mirror to my heart and saying, "Here. This is what your motives *really* are." The heart can be deceptive—we know from Jeremiah 17:9. We can twist our motives and lie about our true intentions and generally fool the world. We can do these things, but we don't have to. We don't have to live that way. We can live lives of truth, lives of transformation, lives at peace. We do these things by staying attached to Christ. John 15 is here to remind us that the spiritual maturity we long for comes only by way of a certain privacy between God and us. It comes only when we quit clawing for control and learn to rest in the enoughness of God. I've discovered firsthand that it is a learned behavior, as opposed to a skill we simply drift toward.

After Pam and I left ministry in Shreveport, Louisiana, and relocated to Amarillo, Texas, where I went to work in radio, I knew in my heart that I would pastor again one day. I wasn't completely sure I wanted to, but I knew deep down that I would. When you're called by God to do something, you're generally aware of what that something is; I knew for sure I'd been called.

Because of the certainty of my call, as soon as we got ourselves settled in West Texas, I began volunteering at a thriving church nearby. They needed help in their singles' department, and so that's the group I chose to serve. Under my leadership, the ministry grew quickly—so much so that one day one of the members of the pastoral staff approached me to say that he and several other senior leaders were leaving that weekend for a ministry retreat and that one of the items on their list of discussion points centered on hiring me to serve full-time. On staff. As the pastor to the singles' group.

I was honored but not all that surprised. I knew how well the department had been doing and also knew, as I've mentioned, that God wanted me to pastor again. You can imagine my shock, then, when this pastor returned from the retreat, asked for a meeting with me, and then proceeded to tell me I *wasn't* getting the job. I didn't show my cards to him, but inside, I was crushed. I wanted the role. I deserved the role. And I had no doubt I was going to be offered the role. Had I been a betting man, I would have gone all-in on my being "the guy."

Not knowing what else to do, I kept walking the same path I was on, working in radio, serving at that church, waiting for things to come to me instead of pushing down doors left and right. It was challenging, this intentional relinquishing of control, but despite a fair amount of kicking and screaming inside, I knew it was the right thing to do.

A few years later, the tiny church in Hereford, Texas, came calling, and asked if I would serve as the senior pastor. I was excited to say yes, but there were aspects of the job that certainly would put me on the back side of the desert. I would be serving in obscurity ... was I really okay with that?

I did say yes to the role, and Pam and I did move to Hereford. And it was indeed like living on the back side of the desert. But we were happy. We were at peace. We were doing what God had asked us to do.

Ironically, it was when I was there in that desert place that a man named Robert Morris came to serve as guest speaker one weekend at our tiny church. He and I stayed in touch after that weekend, and we became fast friends. Eventually, it would be Robert who would hire me to serve with Gateway Church in the Dallas–Fort Worth area, and from there, I'd be asked to serve as the senior pastor at New Life in Colorado. But my point is that I might never have met Robert had the church in Amarillo hired me to be the singles' pastor. The role would have given me greater visibility and would have carried a little more prestige than was attached to the Hereford opportunity. But then I wouldn't have had the benefit of being in the desert for a while, of hiding myself away in God.

In his book *Prototype*, Jonathan Martin wrote, "The only real antidote to the clamor of the crowd is time in the wilderness, where our true identity can be established and we can hear the still, small voice of God."[5]

THE SPOTLIGHT AS CUNNING ADULTERESS

Cycling back to Jesus's experience, I find it intriguing that after spending forty days in the desert, "Jesus returned to Galilee powerful in the Spirit." And "news that he was back spread through the countryside. He taught in their meeting places to everyone's acclaim and pleasure" (Luke 4:14–15).

It's that last part that gets me, the part about his teaching being so well received. If there is one thing we can be sure of from the Scriptures, it is that Jesus lived a sinless life. By extension, this means that he never was boastful, arrogant, or proud. And yet we learn here in Luke that he got all sorts of accolades for bringing down the house when he taught. Moreover, we know from our previous discussion that he often voluntarily withdrew to spend time with God. I think these two things are connected; I think being able to handle praise well in public has a lot to do with embracing obscurity in private, with periodically hiding oneself away in God.

It's a good test, that of seeing how well you do when you're praised publicly, as a determinant of how faithful you've been to hole away with God. Does praise puff out your chest, elevate your self-concept, and make you start to believe your own press? Or does it remind you whose power you're really operating on, the divine set of shoulders on which you truly stand?

We typically overrate ourselves here. We think we, of all people, can handle praise exceptionally well. (Just try us! Really, you'll see!) We beg God for opportunities we're sure we're ready for, big-league chances to finally show our stuff. To which our loving heavenly Father says to each of us, "No, no, child. Chase after anonymity instead. If promotion is ever right for you, then at the right time, *I'll* raise you up. *I'll* provide the avenue for public praise."

The spotlight is a cunning adulteress; we don't believe this, but it is true. But because we don't believe it is true, we continue tooting our own horns. Because we fear God will slack off on his promise to promote us at the right time, we insist on promoting ourselves.

When Pam and I were first married, we were part of a class at church comprising both singles and couples who were roughly our same age. One of the members of that class was a young woman who was very passionate about her relationship with God. She was missions minded and always seemed to be serving or giving or doing, all in the name of Christ. She fit the southern stereotype of hair that was always "done," makeup that was always flawless, and clothing that always matched, which is why it was noticeable when she showed up to a class dinner party one night with no makeup and gross, greasy hair.

Of course we had to ask what had happened to her that would cause her appearance to so radically shift. Had she been on a week-long camping trip? Had she run out of shampoo? Somebody posed the question we all were dying to ask, and she answered, "Oh, well, I am fasting this week. And based on the Scriptures, we are supposed to put oil on our heads whenever we fast."

The verses she was referring to are found in Matthew 6. "But when you fast," verses 17 and 18 read, "put oil on your head and wash your face, so that it will not be obvious to others that you are fasting, but only to your Father, who is unseen; and your Father, who sees what is done in secret, will reward you" (NIV).

Context is helpful here; in Jesus's day, to put oil on one's head and wash one's face was the equivalent of our saying, "Get out of bed. Clean up. Get dressed. Go on about your day as you normally would." What Jesus most definitely was *not* saying was, "Draw attention to yourself and to your sacrificial ways." No, he much prefers subtle types.

We don't prefer subtlety ourselves.

We struggle to tithe because it costs us money. We struggle to pray because it costs us time. We struggle to fast because it costs us focus. And we struggle to do anything that is costly for God, if we aren't sure we'll be recognized for it somehow. Oh, sure, we'll do the thing. But then we'll burn with the need to tell somebody, to review why all this godly grease is all over our hair. We'll refuse to rest until the points get put on our scoreboard, until everyone who may be watching knows just how awesome with a capital *A* we are.

In terms of our strong suit, subtlety isn't it.

We tend to mock the Pharisees of old, and yet we're more like them than we care to admit. They were an impressive religious people who knew the first five books of the Bible by heart. They wore spiritual fervor like a beloved coat and were known to pray— literally—all the time. They probably never missed church. They probably were never even late for church. They followed the law of Moses perfectly, a reality that ought to give us pause. For all our self-promoting grandstanding, have we ever done anything perfectly in all our lives?

The fact is, even the most noble among us would have been in awe of the Pharisees. This was an impressive group of people, and yet Jesus was unimpressed. Why? Because their motives had gone awry. They wore their spirituality not in order to gain intimacy with God but so that they'd gain favor with people. Jesus said, "I appreciate your diligent efforts, but I'm afraid you've missed the point."

Earlier in Matthew 6, we read this:

> Be careful not to practice your righteousness in front of others to be seen by them. If you do, you will have no reward from your Father in heaven. So when you give to the needy, do not announce it with trumpets, as the hypocrites do in the synagogues and on the streets, to be honored by others. Truly I tell you, they have received their reward in full. But when you give to the needy, do not let your left hand know what your right hand is doing, so that your giving may be in secret. Then your Father, who sees what is done in secret, will reward you. (vv. 1–4 NIV)

I don't know about you, but I can barely get past that first line without sinking hip deep into self-reproach. Honestly, I can't conceive of a world in which I don't call attention to myself. Our entire social-media structure is predicated on the idea of calling attention to ourselves. Sure, we can cloak it in all sorts of noble things—prayer requests and praise reports and giving God glory for the good things he has done. But if we're not extremely careful, what we'll be doing is building our own followership instead of his.

True, God says that we are to let our light shine so that people will see our good works and glorify our Father in heaven, and despite appearances on the surface, this is no contradiction to his advice to do all good deeds in secret. What he's saying is to give our motives some thought. Our intentions are to be so pure, so innocent, so Godward in their direction that others will know intuitively it's Christ we're living for.

Still, the question remains: Can we tweet the stuff we want to tweet, or not? I'll leave that to you and God. Yes, testimonies of God's goodness require a voice to speak them (see Rom. 10:14), but perhaps we can do better about running our "testimonies" through a motivation checkpoint first. Are we speaking, posting, tweeting, or otherwise broadcasting things so that people will be impressed with us, or so that they'll be impressed with our God?

The blessing, Jesus says, comes to those who seek to hide themselves away.

WHAT WE FIND ON THE DESERT'S BACK SIDE

The idea of being sent to the back side of the desert used to terrify me: What would I miss while I was gone? But at some point my perspective did shift, and these days I'm finding myself actually craving that time away. The wilderness is becoming my home as much as my study or my back porch; whether for a moment between meetings on a busy workday, or for an entire week, while decompressing on the heels of an intense season of ministry, I go there, and inevitably I learn things about God and about myself while hidden away in his loving arms that I don't seem to learn any other way. "Deserts, silence, solitudes are not necessarily places but states of mind and heart," wrote Catherine de Hueck Doherty, founder of the Madonna House Community. "These deserts can be found in the midst of the city, and in the every day of our lives. We need only to look for them and realize our tremendous needs for them. They will be small solitudes, little deserts, tiny pools of silence, but the experience they will bring, if we are disposed to enter them, may be as exultant and as holy as the one God himself entered. For it is God who makes solitude, deserts, and silences holy."[6]

Precious excavations are made in obscurity; these don't get made while onstage. When I stay attached to the vine of Christ, I sense the Lord's pleasure uniquely. There, I'm reminded who I am. I'm reminded whose I am. I'm reminded it's okay to leave my promotion in his capable hands.

Luke 14 tells of a time when Jesus went to a top Pharisee's house for dinner. Jesus was seated among an entire group of religious scholars when he decided to tell them a story, a story about a dinner party not unlike the one they were enjoying then and there.

"When someone invites you to dinner," he said, "don't take the place of honor. Somebody more important than you might have been invited by the host. Then he'll come and call out in front of everybody, 'You're in the wrong place. The place of honor belongs to this man.' Red-faced, you'll have to make your way to the very last table, the only place left.

"When you're invited to dinner," Jesus continued, "go and sit at the last place. Then when the host comes he may very well say, 'Friend, come up to the front.' That will give the dinner guests something to talk about! What I'm saying is, If you walk around with your nose in the air, you're going to end up flat on your face. But if you're content to be simply yourself, you will become more than yourself."

Jesus then turned to the host, a Pharisee, and said, "The next time you put on a dinner, don't just invite your friends and family and rich neighbors, the kind of people who will return the favor. Invite some people who never get invited out, the misfits from the wrong side of the tracks. You'll be—and experience—a blessing. They won't be able to return the favor, but the favor will be returned—oh, how it will be returned!—at the resurrection of God's people" (vv. 8–14).

I had the joy of watching this type of thing play out in the life of our worship pastor last year. The thing Jon was curious if he could "let go of" was not a grudge or a high-calorie dessert; it was fame. Or maybe, at a minimum, prestige. The trouble is, the guy is great: he is a great singer, a great bandleader, a great songwriter, a great all-around talent. And candidly, he is actually starting to believe that he's great—not in an egocentric way, but in a way that says he understands honest self-assessment, he understands what anointed songwriting looks and sounds like, and he understands the impact thoughtful, God-honoring work has on Christendom.

One of Jon's longtime musical heroes is Martin Smith, of the British Christian rock band Delirious? An occasion presented itself last fall for Jon to sit across from Martin one-on-one and have an earnest conversation about music making, about spirituality, and about success. And during that discussion, the topic of Jon's future came up. In classic Jon style, he was hedging his bets. He is humble as the day is long, and yet he was aware there, as the conversation unfolded, that most likely he was facing a crossroads. His work was becoming known around the country—really, around the globe— but he had local-church responsibilities here at home. Should he leave church leadership and tour full-time? He was already on the road a substantial part of each year; should that become his permanent status now?

He asked Martin for input. He was a good person to ask, really; during his leadership of Delirious?, Smith played in more than forty countries, sang lead and played guitar on seven studio albums, supported bands as diverse as Bon Jovi and Switchfoot, and released songs that led the UK charts several times. If anyone was living Jon's dream, it was Martin. Maybe he'd provide a few pointers on how to navigate the exhilarating ride ahead.

But that's not at all what transpired. There in the café that day, Jon had explained his predicament—he loved leading worship for our church, but the songs he was writing and performing were obviously anointed. Shouldn't he go "chase the dream" God was already making come true? Martin looked at him and said, "My advice to you is to go hide yourself in your church. Serve well in obscurity, and let God promote you at the right time. Don't go pursuing it on your own. The path will make you far less popular, but it will be worth it in the end."

Martin has been honest about his motivations along the way. He led his band for nearly two decades and grew up, morphing from boy to man, there in the public eye. Delirious? disbanded a few years ago, and in a recent interview, Martin reflected on what was going through his mind all that time: "I love doing this for God," he said, "but also I'd really like to be famous, really. You know, nothing we do is pure, is it, in our motive. I think there's always a bit of both going on…. We wanted to be the next U2…. We wanted God to meet people and people to meet God."[7]

This is always the tension as Christ's followers, isn't it? In our heart of hearts, we want to make God famous, even as we crave a tiny little bit of that fame for ourselves.

Jon returned from that trip to the United Kingdom and did the very thing Martin had suggested: he re-upped his commitment here at home. In his words, he began viewing obscure service as "peace, not punishment."

I could stand to take a lesson from this guy.

LIVING RIGHT AND WELL

This morning, as I met with God in prayer, I was asking him about one of the burning desires of my own heart. There is something I believe God has called me to do, and it's something I believe I'm highly gifted to do. And yet that something hasn't unfolded yet. I was throwing a pity party, to put it bluntly. I see other guys being given opportunities left and right to do this thing I believe I'm called and gifted to do, and yet those opportunities aren't coming my way. I told God all of this and then asked, "When is it my turn, God?" to which he said … nothing.

There in the silence, I thought about the "vine and branches" passage in John 15, and about how what pleases God is not what we do—even though this thing is something I really, really want to do—but rather who we are. What pleases him is that we stay close, that we stay hidden away in him. It's true: when Jesus came up out of the waters of baptism at the beginning of his public ministry, God noted that this man was his Son, *in* whom, not *by* whom, he was well pleased.[8] And as much as I sometimes hate to admit it, the same is true for me. It's never my performance God is after—even though I can be pretty good up onstage. It's my praise. And praise requires that I take my focus off myself and place it on what God is up to, on who he is, instead.

He is a God worthy of my praise. Along these lines, Isaiah 42 captures my imagination. It is this God—the one who "created the cosmos, stretched out the skies, laid out the earth and all that grows from it"—who "breathes life into earth's people," who "makes them alive with his own life.

"I am GOD," the passage continues. "I have called you to live right and well. I have taken responsibility for you, kept you safe. I have set you among my people to bind them to me, and provided you as a lighthouse to the nations, to make a start at bringing people into the open, into light: opening blind eyes, releasing prisoners from dungeons, emptying the dark prisons. I am GOD. That's my name. I don't franchise my glory" (vv. 5–8).

And then this, a few verses later, referring to those who choose to stay connected to him: "I'll be a personal guide to them, directing them through unknown country. I'll be right there to show them what roads to take, make sure they don't fall into the ditch. These are the things I'll be doing for them—sticking with them, not leaving them for a minute" (vv. 15–16).

God promises to stick with us when we accept the invitation to stick with him. This is the vine I've chosen. No decision has ever felt so right.

BREAKING BUSY

Challenge #1: Hide Yourself Away

Today, dare to choose obscurity. When the opportunity presents itself for you to offer a kind word, do a good deed, or lend a helping hand, take it. And then comes the hard part: Don't brag about it, tweet about it, tell your spouse or friends about it, or insist in any manner on receiving glory for this very good thing you've done. Pay attention to how you feel hours later, after you've simply treasured up in your heart the beauty you brought to the world around you by serving instead of consuming, and then by letting all forms of self-congratulation simply slip on by.

Challenge #2: Praise God Instead

Whenever you're tempted to self-promote today, focus on promoting God instead. If you find yourself dying to tell all your Facebook friends about the promotion you just received, stop and bow your head and thank God privately instead. When you are jittery with excitement about your kid's latest accomplishment and are about to text all your friends to that effect, stop and bow your head and praise God for your child instead. Let yourself remain in a bit of obscurity today, trusting that God will promote you at just the right time and that his watchful eye is acknowledgment enough.

PART THREE: DETERMINATION
We Live Restored by Practicing Restoration

*Nobody sees a flower—really—it is so small—we haven't
time—and to see takes time, like to have a friend takes time.*

—Georgia O'Keeffe

8

WHAT TO DO ON A DO-NOTHING DAY

Be good, keep your feet dry, your eyes open, your heart at peace, and your soul in the joy of Christ.
—Thomas Merton

HOW TO DO REST RIGHT

Despite the recent busyness battles I've fought of late, people who know me well know I've been on a "rest" kick lately, mostly for the purposes of writing this book. Staff meetings and lunchtime conversations and hallway chats all seem to chase back to this topic of rest, and before I know it, I've climbed back up onto my soapbox, for the umpteenth time, ranting good-naturedly about the dangers of adrenal failure and what we can learn from Sabbath-happy Jews and why whoever said there is no rest for the weary actually had it all wrong.

In response come the questions, all centered on one primary theme. People want to know what a "day of rest" is supposed to include; what it shouldn't include; and whether it has to be a full day, as in twenty-four consecutive hours. They want to know if it's legal to take their kids to soccer practice or run by the grocery store or go to the movies on a day supposedly set aside to think about God.

Regarding making a commitment to a regular bedhead day, or even a bedhead hour, for that matter, it seems the concern is not so much, *How do I do it?* but rather, *How do I do it right?*

Dan Allender, as always, hits home:

> The mandate to rest from our work during the Sabbath is so slight and innocuous that it is boggling to the mind to consider how quickly questions come about how to "do it right." Should the Sabbath begin on Friday at dusk, Saturday, or Sunday at sunrise? Does it need to be twenty-four hours, or could it be morning and a part of an afternoon? Can one drive a car? Get gasoline? Stop for takeout food? Deliver food to a sick friend? Shop online if no one is working? Answer a phone?
>
> The war against delight rages the moment one puts the boundary between the Sabbath and all other time. The war involves guilt and shame-based demands that we "do it right" so no one can accuse our motives or deeds, including God.[1]

To Allender's point, I've noticed that even the most free-spirited among us tend to want to know the score. We want to be assured that if we do X and add Y, then we'll get Z every time. We want to be guaranteed a predictable landing, before we agree to take the plunge.

A couple from church comes to mind. The mom and dad have four kids, all of whom are young adults. Along the way, the parents put the kids through the same strict paces: the kids were home-schooled and allowed only limited involvement in outside activities, such as playing on sports teams or babysitting or hanging out with friends. When the kids reached teenage years, they were allowed only to "court" (instead of date), which, to the parents, meant being *very* selective about who their kids were spending time with, how much time they were spending together, and what they were doing during that "together" time. The parents had been taught a "purity formula" somewhere along the way and decided that as long as they followed it to the letter, their kids would all turn out great.

They'd whittled down parenting to a science, and they intended for each of their four "experiments" to prove their hypothesis right: good training plus good boundaries equals good kid who finds good spouse and has good marriage, each and every time.

The first conversation I ever had with this couple occurred in my office, after they'd requested a meeting about what to do with the disillusionment they were feeling toward God. Their eldest, a son, had been "a perfect child," according to them, and had "submitted joyfully" to the rules and restrictions set for him throughout his life. Thankfully, they said, he courted a "lovely young woman" who also appreciated what they referred to as "our way of life." The son wound up marrying the lovely young woman, which pleased this couple to no end. Their formula had worked! Good training plus good boundaries equals good kid who finds good spouse and has good marriage. How we love it when everything adds up.

But everything *didn't* add up.

Six months into the marriage, the "good spouse" had an affair—a bad thing, by anyone's standards—and left the good son for good.

The parents of the good son now sat across from me, tears pooling in both sets of eyes. "This has been the most disappointing season of our lives," the mother began. "I mean, we followed all the principles …"

A colleague of mine was in the meeting with me, and as soon as he and I heard those words, we shared a knowing glance. This couple had done what we all tend to do: we reduce the human experience down to formulas, forgetting that life won't be contained in simple math.

What this man and his wife were saying was, "God owes us better than this result. X plus Y is *supposed to equal Z.*"

WE WANT FREEDOM, WE THINK

As it relates to the idea of living rhythmically, too many people inside the church link arms with the formula-happy crowd. Once they're convinced a bit of rest might do them some good, they rush headlong into the undeniably *nonrestful* practice of crafting—and then enforcing—a daunting list of "thou shalt nots" and "thou shalts." They determine that rest should mean THIS and only THIS and not THAT, especially not THAT.

It's a tightrope walk God never intended us to walk; in fact, it's legalism at its worst.

Legalism is believing God is demanding something impossible of us, something we'll never in a million years achieve. It is the bar set too high, the speed set too fast, the expectations set too lofty, the boundaries set too tight. It is spiritual suffocation. It is darkness when we're desperate for light.

I mow my lawn on many a day of rest and think nothing of the act; come to think of it, some of my most sacred moments with God have occurred while perched on that fat riding-mower seat. But I know people who get jittery when I reveal this "dark secret" of mine. Internally, I always have the same reaction: *Seriously? You're up in arms over this?*

Yes, in fact, they are. Not only are they convinced a divine demerit is headed my way, but they're also convinced I deserve it. They're legalists, through and through, whether they choose to admit it or not.

My advice to us all—the legalists, as well as those like me, who shake our heads in astonishment at the restrictions legalists choose to rig up—is simply to live free. Be free. Focus on enjoying your rest. Keri Wyatt Kent wrote, "Here's what Jesus seemed to be saying with his actions: 'You've heard it said to keep the Sabbath holy, which you've done by avoiding certain tasks. But I say to you, "Keep the Sabbath by engaging in relationship, by restoring people to community, to wholeness, by *setting people free*."'"[2] (And I'd add: "We might try starting with ourselves.")

This is why people were outraged with Christ while he was here on planet earth, because he compromised rules to champion relationship. He healed on the Sabbath, remember? He also fed people on the Sabbath, trumpeted the coming kingdom on the Sabbath, and did all sorts of things on the Sabbath that the rule-keeping Pharisees said he shouldn't do. He was the perfect embodiment of being free, living free, and focusing on enjoying his rest.

We try to follow suit and all too quickly realize this Jesus pace is harder than we think. We don't really know what to do with freedom. Can we trust ourselves? What if we fail? Like a toddler who has just learned to toddle, we think, *The only way I'll know I'm out of bounds here is when somebody big yells, "No!"*

"This may be one of the reasons we are so averse to play and prefer the tedium of work," wrote Allender. "Freedom scares us. We demand freedom, yet we fear the risk required to recreate in a manner that has such openness, vulnerability, and potential for failure."[3]

We want freedom—yes. But will we know what to do with it once it's ours?

- - - - - - - - - - - - - -

Thankfully, Jesus knows how to steward freedom well. And in typical fashion, he didn't hoard the information, keeping the secrets to life to himself; instead, he put on flesh, came to planet earth, and asked us to taste head-to-toe liberation for ourselves.

Upon close examination, I find that all of Jesus's "commands" were actually invitations in disguise. Granted, they are framed in a commanding voice—"Repent." "Follow me." "Let your light shine." "Honor God's law." "Keep your word." "Go the second mile." "Love your enemies." "Seek God's kingdom." "Do not judge." "Take my yoke." "Honor your parents." "Deny yourself." "Forgive offenders." "Be a servant." "Be born again." "Feed my sheep." "Make disciples." … the list goes on. But based on John 14:15, these "commands" are actually based in love. "If you love me," the verse says, "show it by doing what I've told you." We follow Jesus's injunctions because *Jesus* is the one we love.

But like so many other plainly true things, we don't believe this truth is true. We get to the thing about coming to him when we are "weary" so that he can "give [us] rest" (Matt. 11:28 NIV), and we think, *Command! I don't like commands! Quit telling me what to do!* when in fact we should be thinking, *Invitation. This is an invitation.* More specifically, *This is a God-given gift.*

RECEIVING REST AS A GIFT FROM GOD

Whenever I catch a whiff of Sabbath-keeping legalism in someone I'm talking to, I encourage him or her with this very advice, to start treating rest not as a command but as a gift. "This ought to be task number one on your restfulness to-do list," I tell the person. "I mean, if you're going to have a list, then this should be at the top."

A gift is something everybody likes. Who can refuse a gift? When someone offers to buy me a nice meal, for instance, or I've been invited to use a friend's beach home, or I get an unexpected treat in the mail, these things don't exactly add stress to my life. They make me exhale, they make my shoulders fall, and they make me smile. The effect is the very opposite of stress, which is the point exactly. This is how it goes with a gift and how it ought to go with rest.

A recent Saturday, when Pam and our kids were in Louisiana visiting family, was this type of gift for me. I had helped lead a youth conference at our church all week that culminated with a wonderfully inspiring worship service Friday night. The experience was fantastic, but by Saturday morning, I was toast. I woke later than usual—seven thirty, I think it was—and as my eyes blinked opened and my mind came to, I thought, *This day of rest—this is a gift.*

I thanked my Father aloud: "God, thank you for this gift."

I missed my family, but I received the time as a gift. A gift is something to be opened and savored. A gift is something to enjoy. I drank coffee and read and prayed and read some more. I leaned in as God revealed some areas of my heart that needed work, and I thanked him for showing me two specific ways I could be a better dad to my two amazing kids. I took a hike. Literally. And continued to talk with God. Then, after showering and dressing, I drove down to Whole Foods to shop for something to eat. The guy manning the seafood counter said they'd just that afternoon received some shrimp, fresh from the Gulf—"It's pretty rare we get these," he said. Done. Dinner was decided there on the spot.

The cooking process was slow but effective, and a few hours later, I set before myself a plate of home-cooked Cajun shrimp, at which point I thanked God profusely for edible ocean life.

It had actually been my intention to go slow, to clean and devein and sauté and prepare … I'd wanted this to be an event, not a task. And it was. And my heart was full because of it. Fourteen solid hours of wake time, and not a single minute was rushed. What's more, nothing of measurable value was accomplished, no task list was completed, no ambition was promoted, no production whatsoever to report. It was sweet time with God—no agenda, no real outcome, nothing except fellowship with him.

Progress, to be sure.

The following day was intense due to the departure of a beloved member of our staff team who took a role in another church, and then I had scheduled a rigorous day of writing that Monday. I remember driving home Monday evening, thinking, *Even after the last two days, I still have something left in the tank.* I had filled up so much on Saturday—emotionally, spiritually, mentally, and physically—that I was sort of skipping through my week. Well, not skipping—I wouldn't picture a field of daisies, exactly. But I certainly felt less burdened. I wasn't weighed down as I sometimes am. Rest had yielded good returns. For so long I refused to buy into that idea, but it was proving to be the truth. Receiving rest as a gift is not unlike conducting a spiritual "Where's Waldo?" search—you know those red-and-white stripes are somewhere; you just have to seek them out.

I was getting ready for bed last night and heard the soft whap-whap-whap of rain falling on the roof. I'm a sucker for a good rainstorm, and so I beelined it for the back deck, settled into a comfortable chair there under the eaves, and watched the drama unfold. Vibrant lightning. A cool wind. Thunder rumbling off in the distance. I grinned as I imagined God with a conductor's wand in hand, orchestrating the entire show. The performance was gone as quickly as it had started, but I was there to see it. What's more, I saw it not merely as condensation falling to earth, but I saw it as a gift.

I feel the same way each spring when I catch sight of the season's first robin redbreast. Or when I detect those tiny buds finally bursting through the beds of mulch. *Gift.* Each one a bona fide gift.

When I was with Eugene and Jan Peterson at their Montana home, Eugene took me on a walk along the perimeter of his property. A mutual friend once told me that Eugene could name and give the origin of every single plant on his grounds, and what I was seeing were a *lot* of plants. Who is that tuned-in to his surroundings? Of course, it is someone who lives life at rest.

And so I pay attention as I rest. Or I try to pay attention, anyway. I try to slow down, to look around, to take in with grateful eyes the immediate world in which I live. On this topic of paying attention, of silencing all distractions in favor of tuning into God and his handiwork, author Rachael Held Evans once wrote, "My inner voice can be a royal pain in the rear. An obstreperous child, impatient with questions and eager for attention, my inner voice likes to focus on the future, not the present, and already she had some rather strong opinions about lunch. 'Quiet, quiet, quiet,' I kept telling myself. 'Embrace the silence. Focus on God.' But nothing seemed to work. My mind kept drifting from one thing to another, and before I knew it, I was outlining an article in my head. Finally, I remembered something my agent told me before I left for this retreat. 'When you're on the [spiritual] retreat,' she said, 'don't try too hard to make something mystical happen. Just go and *be*. If you enter with too many expectations, you'll be disappointed.'"

Reflecting on that time away, she later said, "So what did God say to me in the silence that morning? I'm not sure, but I think it was something like, *Don't try so hard, little child*, and *Hey, check out this cool turtle I made*."[4]

You "receive the gift" when you listen to yourself breathe. It happens when you put down the phone or close the laptop or cease tweeting for even ten seconds and open your ears to a neighbor needing to talk. It can happen when you watch your teenage son shuffle toward the refrigerator, grab the OJ from the shelf, take a swig right from the carton, and then sheepishly smile as he turns and sees that he's been caught. You halfheartedly shake your head in response and grin, thinking not thoughts of indictment, of frustration, but of grateful disbelief that he's gotten so big.

It happens when you make time to appreciate a splendid and too-short rainstorm. It happens when you hold your spouse close and whisper, "I love you," into a ready ear. It happens when you live out a passage of Scripture you've read with mild indifference a dozen times.

And yes, it happens when you notice the turtle paddling along, there in the gurgling creek.

When you're looking, you will find them, these astounding gifts from God. And when you open up a hand to receive them—that's when you get rest right.

THANKING GOD FOR THE GIFT OF REST

After a wildfire in our neighboring community of Black Forest, more than five hundred homes were deemed "total losses," twenty-five of them owned by families who are part of our church.

One couple in their sixties lost everything except the clothes on their backs. They were relieved to have escaped alive, but as you'd expect, they felt naked without any of their "things." No toothbrushes, no underwear, no spare pairs of shoes. None of their computers, none of their photo albums, none of their socks or towels or books. Sure, these things could all be replaced, but for the three-week period following their evacuation, life for them felt empty and barren and sad. All their systems had been disrupted; everything familiar to them was now gone.

The couple fled to the home of good friends—close friends, friends who take you in when everything has been lost—who lived several miles south of the burn area. This is what the church does during crisis: we rally to meet the needs we find.

So, this pair appeared on the doorstep—separately, because the wife had been at the gym working out and the husband had been at work before making a mad dash to their home, grabbing their cat and two dogs, and then racing back up his street—and they said, "We have no way of knowing if our house will make it, but we've been evacuated for the foreseeable future, until fire-safety personnel can get in there, do an assessment, and let us know what's next."

Before they could make their actual request—"Can we stay in your guest room for a while?"—their friends hugged them and ushered them inside and said, "What's ours is yours. Stay as long as you like." They then pointed the jittery couple toward the spare bedroom, invited them to use the fresh towels in the bathroom cabinet if they wanted to clean up, and said that dinner was already under way and that there was plenty to go around.

As I mentioned, it was a full three weeks before the couple was able to find a house to rent, somewhere to call "home," because theirs had, in fact, burned to the ground. And during that twenty-one-day period, sorrow would wash over them like the never-ending waves of the sea. One moment they'd be mourning the decades-old family portraits they'd never be able to replace, and the next they'd find themselves laughing over the general amusements of daily life. They'd feel buoyed by the momentary uplift, the smiles, only to be knocked down by the next wave of grief. It was exhausting, the wife later admitted, but still they found a way to cope.

Each evening, after dinner but before everyone was weary and ready for bed, the four adults would gather on the back deck, and there beside the flickering flame of a candle, they'd recount God's faithfulness from the day. At first, it was slim pickings: "Well, we had to go meet with our insurance agent," the husband might say, "and while there is a ton of red tape involved in a situation like this, our agent said, probably in passing, 'I'm sorry for your loss.' It was a trivial thing, I guess. But today it felt like a gift from God."

They'd go on this way for fifteen or twenty minutes—no more than that, most nights—speaking aloud the gifts they believed were from the hand of God: a good night's sleep the previous night, an extension on a work deadline, news that another neighbor was safe and sound, the generosity of loving friends. And then they would blow out the candle and get ready for bed, and gear up to tackle the trying tasks the next day surely would bring.

It takes a special sort of strength to thank God for the gift of rest, especially when rest doesn't feel like a gift. For this couple, life had tossed a set of circumstances their way they absolutely did not want. And yet even there, in the ambiguity and frustration and pain, they viewed the three-week period of rest as a gift. And they thanked God for that gift.

Thankfulness works magic on a harried heart. When we insist on being grateful, on seeking out places to point our praise, our rhythms can't help but right themselves. Our heart rates can't help but come down.

- - - - - - - - - - - - - - -

I got my professional start in journalism and remain an admirer of stars in the field, one of the brightest of whom is Pulitzer Prize–winning investigative journalist Katherine Ellison. According to her official bio, in addition to authoring four books and serving both as a foreign correspondent and, later, as a writing consultant, Ellison has "traveled underground with Eritrean guerrillas fighting the Ethiopian government, reported from the front lines of U.S.-backed wars in Central America, hunted for Nazis in Paraguay and Argentina and spent a week traveling with a band of Huichol Indians during their annual ceremonial peyote hunt in central Mexico. She has been taken hostage by Mexican peasants, arrested by Cuban police, tear-gassed in Panama, chased by killer bees and required to watch more World Cup events than she cares to remember."[5]

The woman has been busy. And yet you get the feeling from reading one of her latest books, *Buzz: A Year of Paying Attention*, that more chaotic than all these episodes put together has been the chaos of raising a clinically distracted son.

Ellison's son, whom she and her husband nicknamed "Buzz" for his always frenetic energy, was diagnosed with ADHD as a child, plunging the couple into a difficult and demoralizing world. Across his adolescent years, Buzz was often angry, sometimes violent, and always misunderstood. He chased off all his childhood friends and most of his younger brother's friends; finally reaching a breaking point, Ellison considered boarding school or some other sort of long-term option that would get Buzz out of the house. She even revealed the plan to her son on the heels of one especially frustrating afternoon, explaining with tight lips and a serious tone, "You will *not* destroy this family."

What Ellison didn't realize early on was that her own "clinical distraction"—she, too, had been diagnosed with an attention deficit disorder along the way—was feeding the beast of her son's disobedience. She wrote, "An innately challenging child can easily wear down the average parent, and in particular the scatterbrained parent. The child's extraordinary resistance leads that parent either to back off or resort to harsh punishment, making the child even more angry and aggressive. And so on, and so on, until everything falls apart."[6]

Armed with this new insight, and still desperate for relational relief, the Ellisons seized every opportunity for healing they could find, including everything from "medication to meditation; cognitive therapy to powdered soy shakes; neurofeedback, hair analysis, genetic testing, special diets, and summer camps dedicated to organizational skills."[7] They also tried custom exercise routines, tinted contact lenses, horseback therapy, and swimming with dolphins. She jokes that with a little more time and an ounce more exasperation, exorcism would have been next on their list.

Still, at the end of it all, Buzz was still Buzz, complete with his anger, his cynicism, and his grief. And the fractured family was still writhing in pain. Clearly, something drastic needed to be done; the question, she and her husband feared, wasn't *if* something tragic would become of the Ellisons as a result of Buzz's issues, but *when*.

It's widely known in ADHD circles that kids who suffer from the disorder face some pretty sobering statistics. They have, for example, "four times as many car accidents as those who aren't affected. They have five times the rate of suicide attempts, and ten times as many teen pregnancies. They're also more than twice as likely to be arrested, and up to three times as likely to abuse alcohol and drugs." What's more, the disorder in children has been linked to "significantly higher rates of divorce by their parents, and to a greater chance that the children will be physically abused. It may be invisible from the outside, but the suffering it causes is all too obvious."[8]

Ellison had a solution in mind. Rather than pay for additional medical and psychiatric interventions, she would simply pay attention to her son. She would apply her investigative journalist's eye to the struggling young man living under her own roof and see what she could learn. She would slow down, step back, let go of her expectations, and take in life through a totally different lens.

She did this not for a day or a week, but for a full year, her observations forming the spine of her book. Once she had hindsight on her side, she would say, "If I've learned anything by now, it's that kids like Buzz do best with parents who aren't having tantrums right back at them, or even frantically checking e-mail every five minutes—parents able to listen closely and explain things patiently and repeatedly. Yet this sort of self-control so easily eludes me when I'm in my default mode of scrambling around in frustration over projects left up in the air."[9]

And so she would practice—practice listening closely and explaining things patiently and generally avoiding the chain reaction that tumbles forth when a parent responds angrily, judgmentally, to a child. "I've come to believe that the only way to break this chain," she said, "is to keep in mind William James's idea that what you pay attention to becomes your reality and, whenever possible, to keep my focus fixed on the best parts of people's natures."[10]

Ellison's newfound focus paid off. Things didn't go perfectly, but while the relationship is still admittedly a work in progress, she describes it as "restored." She explains: "I know I've already seen glimpses of the gifts Buzz may one day unwrap.… Somewhere inside my son, I'm learning to trust, there's a *good* man, just trying to get out."[11] And she chooses to pay attention to that goodness, to the host of things she is learning that she might not have learned, had she parented an easier kid.

As strange as this may sound, I bring this up not as a parenting example but as a paying-attention example for both you and me. The truth is, I read Ellison's story and found myself relating a little too well. I may never have been diagnosed with "clinical distraction," but I've been plagued with distraction of the spiritual sort for years—and I believe it is no less severe. Sure, maybe I can mask my dysfunction better, presenting a more socially acceptable front, but still it lurks under the surface, causing me to embrace chaos as readily as Buzz.

I look back on old patterns with disgust—the overworking that almost cost me my marriage, the blatant disregard for the feelings of close friends, the mental hopscotch that has sabotaged so many times of study and prayer—and I consider how weary I became in doing good. The Bible says not to do that, and now, all these years later, I think I know why. *Margin* author Richard Swenson says that whenever he confronts Christians about their out-of-control pace of life, he braces for the response he most often gets, which is some iteration of Philippians 4:13: But I can do all things through Christ who strengthens me. Richard wants to ask, "Can you? Can you fly? Can you go six months without eating? Neither can you live a healthy life chronically overloaded."[12]

I'm not sure I ever really gave Christ such "credit" for my pressure-cooker pace, but I certainly subscribed to the "I can do all things" way of life. And did I ever learn the hard way that nobody can do everything—at least not without paying a steep price.

At last I recognize my "bedhead days" for what they are: no less than salvation, through and through. Pulling away to enter the rest of God isn't a fun little hobby I can afford to do without. As Ellison discovered, paying attention—keen, heartfelt attention—is the key to living sanely in an insane world. It's the only way the chaos gets calmed. The formula junkies who prod me for day-of-rest dos and don'ts miss the point entirely. It's not the rules, but the relationship. If you're genuinely, lovingly paying attention to God in your rest, the rest of what you do (or don't do) doesn't matter at all.

BREAKING BUSY

Challenge #1: Thank God

You've had several opportunities to practice healthy, rhythmic living to this point—both for an entire day and also throughout the course of your typical daily life. Hopefully you've seized those opportunities and benefited from them. The challenge this time around is for you to acknowledge the One who provides real rest in the first place, your heavenly Father. As you experience moments of Shabbat shalom this week, quiet moments when you can actually breathe, when the frenetic pace of life is divinely kept at bay, thank God for the gift of rest. You might whisper a prayer, jot down a journal entry, or simply look skyward and say thanks. Let him know you are aware of the gift he's providing and that you're actually receiving it in the spirit with which it came.

Challenge #2: Find Your Buzz

Just as Katherine Ellison saw great gains in her relationship with her son when she ceased trying to fix him and instead simply paid attention to the goodness embedded in him, his realities, and his needs, you, too, can realize significant benefits by training your eye, your energy, and your attention on the positive aspects of a part of your life that feels broken or wounded or raw.

For this challenge, choose the object of your dissatisfaction—a key relationship, a seemingly immovable obstacle at work, your weight, your bank account, whatever—and note what you observe. What causes you pain there? Why is the situation so tough?

Now, write down something positive about the circumstance or relationship, some aspect of goodness that still remains. What steps can you take this week and this month to build on that goodness you've declared? Consider asking a friend to hold you accountable to taking those steps sooner rather than later.

9

THREE THINGS I WISH I'D KNOWN

Sometimes I lie awake at night and ask, "Where have I gone wrong?"
Then a voice says to me, "This is going to take more than one night."
—Charles M. Schulz

AVOIDING PITFALLS ALONG THE ROAD TO REST

I've been a pastor for nearly two decades now, and throughout this time, I've been the product of on-the-job training. Maybe every job is this way. Do you know any good doctors or lawyers or teachers or artists who quit learning years ago? I don't either. Nor do I know any good pastors who aren't continually refining their craft. So, while I'm not opposed to having to learn as I go, having to fight to stay a half step ahead of the congregation I've been tasked with leading, having to study and read and restudy and reread so that I can provide something worthwhile come Sunday morning, there are a handful of things I wish somebody had told me before I got started, things I didn't have to learn the hard way.

Things like this: no matter how hard I try, I'll always be tempted to measure my success by my church's attendance numbers. Or, the best thing I can do for my congregation is to quit comparing myself to other pastors and simply strive to be genuinely me. Or, because it takes a long time to become "old friends," I ought to nurture and cherish the old friendships I have. Or, I will only be given as much spiritual authority as the amount of spiritual authority I'm willing to submit to. Or, my brain will always, always feel like scrambled eggs on Sunday afternoon and again all day Monday; I will do well to hold all decisions until Tuesday. Or, I will never regret spending time with my family. Or, while it's true that sheep bites can't kill me, the general congregational gnawing every pastor is made to withstand will make life absolutely miserable a few (very long) days each year.

Granted, when you learn the hard way, the lessons get ingrained in you like the brand on cattle's behinds. But I doubt any cow would describe that process as fun. No, personally I'd recommend the easy way out. I'm more stubborn than the average guy, so in reality, people probably did tell me the things I needed to know, all those years ago. Most likely I just didn't have ears to hear. My spirit probably revolted, thinking, *I'll figure it out on my own, thank you very much.* Only I doubt I actually said thanks.

Perhaps you're the same way. If you have a bit of "driver" in your personality, a smidge of type A behavior in how you roll, then you, too, will insist on learning the hard way. You will be one of the growing group of people who have learned-the-hard-way horror sto-ries to tell—about odorless gas leaks, about rottweilers and children, about weekend warriors and ACL surgery. And about nearly killing yourself before you learned to appreciate rest.

If, however, you're a less stubborn person (or even a stubborn one who happens to be in a teachable mood), then this chapter is for you. The three things I wish I'd known long ago, but didn't, might help you avoid a pitfall or two along the path to living a rhythmic life.

NO. 1: REST IS OPPOSED

The first rhythmic-life lesson I learned the hard way is this: our rest is opposed. During the early days of my marriage, when I was running too fast and pushing too hard, I found it incredibly difficult to "come down." I feared rest. I feared the loneliness and boredom I knew rest would usher in. And so I kept the pedal to the metal, upping my RPMs higher and higher, while praying each and every moment that I'd somehow avoid a crash.

But the reality is that we always have to come down. We can't stay up forever. And because I refused to learn how to slow myself in a healthy manner, I was forced to walk an unhealthy path, a path paved with Internet porn. From a place of deep humility, I have shared with my congregation how challenging it was to untangle myself from the grip of pornography across the span of several years in my twenties, but by God's grace, I did get free.

For quite a while, I looked back on that stretch of sinfulness with disbelief; how could I stoop to that level? I was in ministry. I was supposedly living for God. I adored and admired my wife. And yet, still, I'd find myself sitting in front of a computer screen, long after Pam had gone to bed, staring at stuff I had no business staring at, regretting the minutes even as they ticked by.

Things make more sense to me now. When you and I don't say yes to God's form of rest, we will say yes to a fraudulent form of rest, cooked up by the Enemy of our souls. We will say yes to porn or to booze or to drugs or to gambling or to idle chatter or to extravagant spending—all in the name of "unwinding." This is what we'll declare, anyway, when pressed to justify our sinful ways. It's all proof that real rest is opposed, that rest without God is not "rest" at all. My friend John Eldredge likes to say, "Caring for your heart is the first blow against the Enemy's schemes,"[1] and he's absolutely right. Satan hates it when we truly "come down"—in a good and godly way—because that's when spiritual transformation happens. That's when soulish growth takes place. That's when we become like God.

I've long been fascinated with the American Civil War and recently caught a PBS documentary on the Battle of Gettysburg, aired in conjunction with the 150th anniversary of the campaign. Gettysburg happened almost exactly at the halfway point of the four-year war and is considered by many historians to be the turning point for Union forces, who would defeat the Confederacy in the end.

As I watched the reenactment of the specific scenes that made up this battle—Robert E. Lee's high-flying spirits as he marched his troops into Pennsylvania; both sides' strategic use of ridges, town streets, and hills to sneak up on and take down opposition soldiers; the Union's ability to hold their lines despite suffering a ridiculous number of casualties; Meade's defeat of Southern attacks, which would end Lee's invasion of the North—I was intrigued not only by the sweeping maneuvering but also by the utter minutia involved. So many microscopic actions, reactions, decisions, determinations, and declarations—so many tiny things that added up to something huge in the end, something that looked a lot like victory. The Confederates had every opportunity to win the war there at Gettysburg, but they did not. For the Union army, tending to the minor details meant a major win in the grand scheme of things, which leads me to my point.

When we recognize that real rest is opposed, that the Enemy absolutely hates it when we unwind in a godly way, we realize that we, too, are at war. It's a war, and the spoils are our souls. And yet tiny disciplines can yield the biggest of wins.

I'm reminded I'm at war when my family finally sits down for dinner—to pray, to eat, to relax—and someone's phone rings. Or when I get all settled on the back deck for half an hour of solitude with God and my kids choose *then* to be chatty. Or when I set aside a day for hiking and communing with God and a freak snowstorm blows into town. Or when I block off a weekend on the calendar to stay home, without any to-dos, and unwind from a harried pace, and out-of-state friends decide to come to Colorado for a visit. Or when I actually plan a whole week of vacation and I catch a vicious flu bug the morning of day one. All these things have happened to me, and they'll happen again and again. Why? Because we're at *war*. And the Enemy hates to lose.

I begin to win the war, battle by battle, incident by incident, one seemingly innocuous campaign after another, when I silence the phone and keep my family's dinnertime conversation afloat; when I embrace my kids there on the back deck, tend to their immediate needs, and then tell them I'll be with them in twenty minutes or so; when instead of cursing that freak snowstorm, I watch with awe as it blows through; when I carve out an hour on day two of my houseguests' visit to pull away, to retreat alone with God; and when I laugh in the face of vacation-time illness, instead of allowing it to derail my entire week.

Remember the scene we looked at in an earlier chapter, when Jesus told the wind and the waves to be still? This was actually the second time Jesus had withdrawn for a little solitude but was quickly summoned back to his disciples to save the day. Both times, natural storms interrupted his rest. This is the way it always goes, even for Jesus Christ. Something always interrupts our rest, because real rest is always opposed. The old Scotsman Sir James Matthew Barrie—the one who created Peter Pan—once quipped in his charming Anglo-Saxon style, "Has it ever struck you that the trouts bite best on the Sabbath? God's critturs tempting decent men."

I'm willing to concede the point that Satan isn't behind every sidetracking scheme; sometimes maybe it really is just a mischievous fish. Either way, I've learned that unless I commit myself to minding my mind, I defer to the distraction every time.

A few years ago, I experienced a dramatic case of letting distraction rule my days. I was going through a rough patch relationally with another pastor, and over the course of several months, I noticed that whatever free time I had—in the early morning, between meetings, during my drive home—I'd use up by imagining conversations with this person. I'd replay in my mind the last exchange we'd had, and then I'd play out what I wanted to say next, as well as how I thought he'd respond.

In his book *Social Intelligence*, author Daniel Goleman (who also wrote the bestseller *Emotional Intelligence*) said that "rehashing our social lives may rate as the brain's favorite downtime activity,"[2] which tells me I'm far from alone in this regard. We fondle our social relationships, turning them over again and again in our minds. We revisit memories, we plot future exchanges, we wish for do-overs where we come across as witty and wise. And while there is nothing inherently wrong with this practice, it sure does siphon unassigned time.

During the specific occurrence I mentioned, my motivations were actually pretty pure. I wasn't intending to waste time; I was hoping to redeem a relationship. But the fact of the matter was that I was using all my energy having imaginary conversations with a man rather than investing it more prudently by having actual conversations with God.

One morning in my office, when I had headed over to my credenza for a fresh cup of coffee, I sensed God saying, *You know, you're giving a lot of mental space to this, even though the conversations you're envisioning are never going to transpire.*

In response, I said, "You're right."

Admittedly, it was a brief exchange. God was right, and I knew it; I needed to start minding my mind.

Later, I talked to the entire staff about what had happened, explaining that spinning our wheels over virtual conversations only serves to stir us up, while bringing our challenges to God calms us down and puts our anxious thoughts to rest. I didn't mandate anything to our staff that day, and I didn't have to. Lectures, diatribes, and strict enforcement of rules pale in comparison to the power of sheer truth.

To this issue of minding our minds, I once heard a story of a monk who, in the course of everyday life, periodically rang what's called a "mindfulness bell." People nearby who heard the bell would stop what they were doing and take three silent, mindful breaths. Then they would continue their work, awakened ever so slightly by the simple act of pausing, of breathing, of practicing mindfulness.

I love this idea. And it's more practical than we may first think. I vote for ringing a mindfulness bell throughout our days, whether we have an actual bell or not. Maybe the "bell" is the instant your feet hit the floor in the morning. Or maybe it's each time you slip behind the wheel of your car. Maybe you set a bell chime as your ringtone, and thus it sounds each time you receive a call.

The "bell" could be sitting down to a meal or kissing your spouse at the end of the day or every time you stop to pray. With a little creative thought, you and I can come up with some reminder to focus our thoughts, to mind our minds, to choose to rest in God. The great Vince Lombardi once said, "Winning is a habit," an idea that transcends the world of sports. We practice taking every thought captive because minor habits really do wind up equaling major wins in the end.

NO. 2: RUTHLESSNESS IS REQUIRED

A second lesson I wish I hadn't had to learn the hard way is that when it comes to rest, ruthlessness is required. Living rhythmically may sound like a breezy proposition, but to execute it well, we have to stand our ground.

About eighteen months ago, I called together the most senior leaders of New Life Church. These are the men and women who report directly to me, the ones who oversee every ministry within our church. It's a great group of people—visionary minds, expansive hearts, and hands ever ready to serve. But due to a string of crises and personnel changes—not to mention the nation's economic down-turn that affected every church across this land—our shared working relationship had fallen off track.

As a leader, I'm a big fan of delegation, of trusting the team, of giving away all the control I don't actually need—all things my senior staff is well aware of. But situations beyond our control had forced us to up the ante on our communications for more than three years. I asked to be part of decisions I normally wouldn't need to weigh in on, because our circumstances demanded that I did. A founding-pastor scandal, a fatal shooting on your campus, and a fast and furious financial downturn can do that to a group.

But then that three-year period came to a close, and the stress level let up a bit. This would have been terrific news, except that I completely missed the cue that we had clawed our way out of the woods, and so my senior staff kept bringing me what I now instinc- tively believed were junior-level questions, and my frustration level only went up. Unwittingly, I'd neglected to inform them that we had shifted from "crisis mode" to "normal, everyday mode," and all of us were suffering mightily as a result. They were trying to include me in their minutia, and I was expending precious energy fending off their incessant requests.

You'll recall that at various points throughout my life, I had a huge need to be needed, which was fed by work associates' never- ending string of demands. If someone was needed to teach a class, my hand shot up in the air. If someone was needed to drive the bus, I was ready to roll. If someone was needed to launch the ministry, I was the guy to tap. If someone was needed to lead the charge, I was there, fist raised in the air. So it was more than a little gratifying to realize I'd matured enough in my desire for rest that I would turn down all these flattering requests—for my input, for my wisdom, for my direction and counsel and advice: "Brady, what should we do about filling this position?" "Brady, how would you handle this conflict?" "Brady, what are your thoughts on approving this vaca- tion?" "Brady, how should we proceed?"

They were the woodpeckers, and I was the tree. A guy could die from being needed this much! I called the meeting for the purpose of informing them that if they preferred a pastor who was alive, then they would resume handling their own affairs. To which they said, "Um, all due respect, Pastor Brady, but you created this madness you now despise."

They were right, and all of us knew it. We had the discussion about how we'd come through the various crises and now could resume normal operations but not before applauding Pastor Brady for not needing to be needed anymore. Not *every* day, anyway.

There are three things a pastor has to do well—lead, shepherd, and communicate—and I know pastors who love to do all three in equal measure. They can oversee meetings, prep for sermons, and speak until they're blue in the face, and they are delighted the entire time. I am not one of those pastors. I don't love these things. I like these things, and I am somewhat good at these things. But love them? Not so much. At least not in an infinite way. Eventually, I become bored with meetings, weary with studying, and annoyed with hearing my own voice. As a result, I employ all sorts of systemic gymnastics in order to thrive week after week. I delegate meeting authority. I meet with a diverse team for sermon prep. Regarding all manner of goings-on around New Life, I opt out as often as I opt in. I do these things to stay sane. I do these things so that sheer chaos doesn't have its evil way in my life.

This is a godly way to lead, by the way. You can see for yourself by reading Exodus chapter 18. Briefly, Moses had led the Israelites out of slavery in Egypt, a process that involved escaping Pharaoh's clutches, miraculously crossing the Red Sea, worrying over food and water, encountering and defeating the Amalekite army, and frequently wrestling with whether they would choose to trust God.

With the drama and near-death experiences behind them, they were able to set up shop near the mountain of God and establish some semblance of normal life.

Moses's father-in-law, a man named Jethro, got wind of this wild turn of events and decided to pay Moses a visit, to see how things were going. Upon Jethro's arrival, he and Moses exchanged hugs and kisses, and then swapped stories of God's faithfulness over a meal. The next day, it was business as usual, as Moses took his seat "to serve as judge for the people" (v. 13 NIV).

Jethro stood back and watched as his son-in-law stayed in that chair from morning until night, deliberating disputes among the people he led. And then he had to speak up. "What are you doing?" he asked Moses, and Moses responded, "This is my job. I am their judge."

And he was telling the truth. The Israelites would bring every quarrel among them to Moses for resolution, because Moses was the guy in charge. He was the only one who knew the decrees and instructions God wanted enforced. And so they would have an argument. And then they'd come to Moses to explain their argument. And then Moses would tell them, biblically, what to do.

It would have been a fine plan, except that Moses was a man. A mortal man. A man who wasn't Superman. He needed rest and relief as much as the next guy, and this pace eventually wore him out. "The work is too heavy for you," Jethro told him. "You cannot handle it alone" (v. 18 NIV).

This gets back to the can-versus-should argument, doesn't it? Perhaps Moses *could* have done the work, but *should* he have? Of course the answer is no. And so Jethro devised a plan. "Teach them [the people] his decrees and instructions, and show them the way they are to live and how they are to behave," Jethro said. "Select capable men from all the people—men who fear God, trustworthy men who hate dishonest gain—and appoint them as officials over thousands, hundreds, fifties and tens.... That will make your load lighter, because they will share it with you. If you do this and God so commands, you will be able to stand the strain, and all these people will go home satisfied" (vv. 20–23 NIV).

In other words, "Delegate, delegate, delegate." And this is exactly what Moses chose to do. In a momentary flash of brilliance, he chose to be ruthless about getting some rest.

In hindsight, I recognize that living by healthy rhythms requires a ruthlessness many people aren't willing to let play out. We're worried about what others will think. We're afraid we'll come across as unfeeling and cold. We're concerned that if we no longer need to be needed, someday we really *won't* be needed—at all! But really, these fears don't prove warranted in the end. In reality, when we are ruthless about protecting our rest, we free up ourselves to be healthy and free up those around us to live rhythmically too.

You probably remember this country's blue laws, which were most strictly enforced up until the mid-1980s. When I was a kid, on any given Sunday it was illegal in most states in the Union to engage in commerce of any kind. You couldn't buy a pair of shoes to walk to the store; you couldn't buy a package of bacon once you got there; and you couldn't buy a pan to fry it in—*everything* was closed. In many states still today, if it's Sunday, you'll be hard pressed to buy a car from a car dealership, because blue laws in that industry are still in effect.

In our city of Colorado Springs, one car dealership in particular imposes a "blue law" of its own: it's open during the week only, from nine in the morning until six at night, despite most of its target market being unavailable to shop for new cars during those particular hours. One of its managers is a New Lifer, and he explained to me that the owner of the dealership said, "It's more important to me that our staff is home with their families each evening, than if we sell an extra car or two."

Workaholics will shake their heads at this logic, but I wonder if God smiles. Fail to plan and plan to fail, and all that; he prefers our plans to center on him.

There is also a local homebuilder that, like national chains Chick-fil-A and Hobby Lobby, chooses to remain closed on Sundays. They run radio ads throughout southern Colorado explaining that the reason they choose not to be open on arguably the most popular home-purchasing day of the week is that they view it as a nonnegotiable top priority to let their staff worship with their families and rest.

Society tends to mock these people, but in fact they're living by the rhythmic code. As the old cliché goes, burning the candle at both ends proves only that you're not very bright.

As we discussed in the last chapter, the last thing I want to suggest is that legalism will do us any favors; it won't. But what these companies have learned is what I myself am learning: ruthlessness paves the road to reliable rest.

NO. 3: THE REWARD IS THE PRESENCE OF GOD

There's a third lesson I've learned along the way, which is that the reward I'm constantly seeking is the persistent presence of God.

We looked at an extended passage from Matthew 6 a couple of chapters ago that is worth revisiting now. There, Jesus tells his disciples that when they give to the poor or when they pray or when they fast, they should do these things not to be seen by other people but only to be seen by God. He says that if those who love God announce their giving "with trumpets" or shout their prayers from the "street corners" or "look somber" while fasting, then they "have received their reward in full" (vv. 2, 5, 16 NIV). Their reward, in other words, is the fleeting praise of other people.

What he does suggest is doing all these things in secret, thereby trusting God to dole out the rewards. (See Matt. 6:4, 6, 18.)

But what does all this have to do with rest?

I think of the words of Matthew 5: "Blessed are the pure in heart, for they will see God" (v. 8 NIV). And I wonder if Jesus's exhortations in Matthew 6 were intended to form an exhaustive list, or whether—I happen to think this is the case—they were simply examples of righteous acts. I wonder if what Jesus was really saying was, "Whenever you practice *any* discipline of obscurity, let my Father's praise be enough."

I think I expected a marching band to materialize after I started taking rest seriously. "Look at me, everyone! Look how seriously I'm taking God's injunction to rest! I'm a Sabbath keeper, folks, plain and simple—holy and righteous and good." I never would have admitted it publicly, but privately I think I hoped for some shiny angel to appear, to deliver the divine prize package I'd so dutifully earned.

The shiny angel never showed up.

- - - - - - - - - - - - - -

I was talking with a woman I've known for some time who lost her first husband to cancer and whose second husband was recently diagnosed with the same disease. Multiplying the stress in her life is the fact that her older son was arrested for embezzlement and is serving jail time, her younger son is being treated for alcoholism, her granddaughter just lost her newborn baby to SIDS, and the mounting expenses from all these situations leave her financially strained every month.

She's been thinking about this potholed path she's been walking for some time now and wanted to bounce her reflections off me. With earnest eyes, she looked at me and said, "Pastor Brady, I have served God and tithed to his church all my life. Can I ask you a simple question? Where is my reward?"

Her question punched me in the gut. This was no simple issue she'd raised. After such faithfulness on her part, why wouldn't God do his?

I wrapped an arm of comfort around her shoulders and let the question sit unaddressed for the moment. She wasn't really looking for answers right then; she was looking for someone who cared. I thought of how many times I've stood in her shoes, and the memories came flooding back. I watched my mom and dad live by the work-hard code for decades and yet still struggle to make ends meet. I myself was the embodiment of diligence and was still passed over for promotions I deserved. My devoted wife wanted desperately to become pregnant for years but instead found her womb empty month after month.

You and I both have been here, haven't we? In that place of having shown up to do what's ours to do and feeling frustrated that God never came. The burdens never lifted. The trials never abated. The troubles never vacationed. The blessings never arrived.

I squared my shoulders to the dear woman and with gentleness said, "Let's reframe things for a moment, okay? When you leave here, you're headed out to the parking lot, where a car that you own is waiting for you, right?"

She nodded as I went on. "And you're going to drive that car home, to a house you also own, a house that has lockable doors and reliable heat? And then you'll fix dinner, correct? Which will mean that just as is the case every other day of your life, you've eaten three square meals in one day?"

She exhaled a little, having sorted out where I was going with all of this.

"Top 5 percent," I said to her. "You're in the top 5 percent of all the people in the world. If you want to make this about material stuff, then remember you're in far better shape than the other 95 percent."

And yet this wasn't about material stuff; she knew it, and so did I.

What it really was about was the stuff of assurance—of knowing that God hadn't lost her file. And the only way she was going to find her footing here was to slow down, look up, and seek peace. It is in our rest that we regain awareness of God, that we're reminded his nearness is our coveted reward.

When Dallas Willard died in 2013, heaven gained a real champion of the faith. Considered by most people to be an expert on "spiritual formation," he wrote often—and well—on the topic of how we become more like Christ, how we get formed into the newness of life we're promised when we go God's way instead of our own. (See Gal. 2:19–20.) Here is a great example of his writing from *The Spirit of the Disciplines*: "Human life cannot flourish as God intended it to, in a divinely inspired and upheld corporate rule over this grand globe, if we see ourselves as 'on our own'—and especially if we struggle to preserve ourselves that way. When we are in isolation from God and not in the proper social bonds with others, we cannot rule the earth for good—the idea is simply absurd."[3]

The key to flourishing, I think Willard would have agreed, is not the doing away with our problems but rather the drawing near to God. I've certainly found this to be true. You get alone with God, and you realize that what you've magnified to monster status God quickly minimizes to the size of a mouse. He says, "Look, I know you're tangled up in knots over this set of circumstances, but you've got to believe me when I tell you it's okay. Keep coming to me, and I'll show you the way out. It's a path I've already lovingly paved."

Granted, I'm not saying we'll always like the path. What I'm saying is it's where we'll find peace.

This is what that woman needed—her big problems upheld by God's even-bigger hands. It's what we all need, in fact. We all need to be reminded that God is near to us. And that he passionately and protectively cares.

We observe the sacrament of Communion most every weekend at New Life Church. It hasn't always been this way, but for the past year or so, we have made it a priority to remind ourselves of God's presence and power in this way every time we gather to worship. I've noticed something during the past twelve months: It's hard to hustle through the wine and the bread. It's nearly impossible to still the soul when the body is still rushing around. And that's a very good thing. We need to stop. We need to savor. We need to consider his presence enough.

In *The Practice of the Presence of God*, seventeenth-century monk Brother Lawrence wrote of the believer, "If sometimes he is a little too much absent from that *divine presence*, God presently makes Himself to be felt in his soul to recall Him, which often happens when he is most engaged in his outward business. He answers with exact fidelity to these inward drawings, either by an elevation of his heart toward God, or by a meek and fond regard to Him; or by such words as love forms upon these occasions, as, for instance, *My God, here I am all devoted to Thee. Lord, make me according to Thy heart.*"[4]

In other words, God's presence is always there for the taking. This is why we practice Communion with regularity, to tell God once again that we wish to be inwardly drawn to him, that we understand our reward is him.

Several weeks ago following Communion, I prayed a prayer written by Martyn Lloyd-Jones to our congregation:

> Throughout the whole of this day, everything I do, and say, and attempt, and think, and imagine, is going to be done under the eye of God. He is going to be with me; he sees everything; he knows everything. There is nothing I can do or attempt but God is fully aware of it all.[5]

A prayer like this can petrify us—*Yikes! His eye is always on me?*—or we can be uplifted by it. Day by day, I'm learning to choose the uplift. I'm learning to see his presence as my reward.

BREAKING BUSY

Challenge #1: Name Your Three

As you read this chapter, you may have thought about lessons you've learned about rest that you wish you would have known before. Go ahead and list them out—what are your top three takeaways about rhythmic living that, had you known sooner, could have saved you a boatload of pain and grief, and spinning, out-of-control days?

Challenge #2: Keep Your Tank Full

Next, write out your strategy for abiding by those lessons from this moment forward, for living with a tank that is full. For you, it may mean enlisting a friend who will tell you the truth if you start running on empty again. It may mean assigning a consistent prayer time with God each morning, so that you stay clear on priority number one. It may mean scheduling quarterly appointments with a counselor, so that you can stay true to who you say you want to be. It may mean signing off of social media for a while, if the temptation to live distracted is simply too much to take. It may mean crafting something of a personal manifesto regarding breaking your addiction to busy and posting it on your bathroom mirror so that you see it each time you brush your teeth. Whatever will help you keep your commitment to living with a tank that is full, do that thing. And do it now.

10

COME ALIVE

----

*Here is the test to find whether your mission on
Earth is finished: if you're alive, it isn't.*
—Richard Bach

MISSION REQUIRES MARGIN

It's a current take on a tale of old, aimed at kids, I can tell—the animation a dead giveaway here. The video's opening scene depicts five cool-looking, trendily dressed friends sitting around, talking, laughing, and enjoying the view of the mountains. There are two girls, three guys, and a donkey. One of the guys—not the one with the bleach-blond Mohawk … one of the others—sees Jesus approaching from far off and stands up to ask him a question as he nears.

"Teacher, what must I do to inherit eternal life?" he asks, to which Jesus, who is wearing a long-sleeved blue waffle T-shirt, skinny jeans, and flip-flops, says, "What is written in the law. How do you read it?"

"Love the Lord your God with all your heart and with all your soul and with all your strength and with all your mind. And love your neighbor as yourself," says the questioner, the one known as an expert in the law.

"You have answered correctly," says Jesus. "Do this, and you will live."

The guy scratches his head, mulling this over a bit. He was trying to test Jesus, and so he probed a little further: "And who is my neighbor?"

The scene changes, as Jesus in customary form proceeds to answer a question with a story. "A man was going down from Jerusalem to Jericho," he says, "when he fell into the hands of robbers. They stripped him of his clothes, beat him, and went away, leaving him half dead." The man on-screen—shaggy hair, goatee, bloodied white T-shirt, jeans, boots—is now writhing in pain, there on the dirt.

"A priest happened to be going down the same road," Jesus continues, "and when he saw the man, he passed by on the other side. So too, a Levite, when he came to the place and saw him, passed by on the other side." As Jesus narrates, we see both the head-dressed priest and the Levite clad in drab browns come by, take in the man in pain, and continue on.

But then a third passerby, a bald hipster, enters the scene—a Samaritan, Jesus calls him—who came where the man was; and when he saw him, he took pity on him. He went to him and—crouching down—bandaged his wounds, pouring on oil and wine; then he put the man on his own donkey, brought him to an inn, and took care of him. The next day, he took out two denarii and gave them to the innkeeper. "Look after him," the Samaritan said, "and when I return, I will reimburse you for any extra expense you may have."

The scene shifts again, and now we see all three passersby in the same shot—the pious priest, the monkish Levite, and the rather unholy looking Samaritan. Jesus eyes the friends who were sitting around shooting the breeze, hoping to catch Jesus in a dilemma, and asks, "Which of these three do you think was a neighbor to the man who fell into the hands of robbers?"

The expert in the law realizes he has absolutely no way out. "The one who had mercy on him," he said, to which the backward-baseball-cap–wearing Jesus said, "Go, and do likewise."[1]

The man leaves Jesus's presence, turning to walk through a door that has mysteriously appeared there in the desert, turns the knob, and enters our modern-day world, filled with bustling city streets, tall buildings, hungry families, shelterless single moms, crying babies who desperately need a diaper change, and more. A world in need—thousands upon thousands of "neighbors" to have mercy upon.[2]

Much has been made of the parable of the good Samaritan down through the ages, and for good reason. Humans have always had trouble considering others' needs ahead of their own. This isn't merely a twenty-first-century predicament; it's a dilemma as old as the hills.

I read the parable—or in this case see it acted out—now through the lens of the Sabbath, of bedhead days, of rhythm and righteousness and rest. And what I discover is that mission requires margin. I won't help another in need until I first create the space that helpfulness requires.

THE MATH OF REST

The Talmud—Judaism's central text—contains an interesting teaching on the Sabbath, which is that if everyone were to observe two Sabbaths in a row, two "bedhead days," in our vernacular, then the Messiah would come immediately and all of humanity would be redeemed.[3]

Now, before you fire off an email accusing me of heresy, I'll quickly acknowledge that the when, where, and how surrounding the second coming of the Messiah remain a mystery to us all, and that, according to Matthew 25:13, we do not know "the day or the hour" (NIV) when we will see him, which is why we're supposed to be prepared at all times for his return. Yes, yes, yes; duly noted.

And yet I think the Talmud is on to something here. I think the seemingly heretical and admittedly brazen statement says *exactly what it means to say*: if we as a people actually practiced rest—consistently, wholeheartedly, in unrelenting fashion—stuff would get restored in and around us that won't be restored any other way. In this manner, wrote Joe Lieberman, "The Sabbath has the power to mend the breach that separates human beings from each other and from God, and that closing those two breaches will create the conditions for redemption."[4]

Which brings me back to the Good Samaritan. Because one man decided to live rhythmically, another man's life was saved. It's math that ought to compel us toward rest: *one helper plus one who is helped equals two lives lived restored.*

When I compare myself to the Good Samaritan, I feel a little inferior, truth be told. Sure, maybe he didn't wake that morning thinking, *I believe I'll hunt for an outreach opportunity today*. But I'll guarantee you this much: he had margin to offer to God. He had left enough margin in his schedule, in his spending patterns, and in his soul, that he could be used in a missional way.

This hardly computes in a Western mind: How can we be expected to do something for someone else when we can barely do what our own lives demand?

I don't have to look beyond the guy staring back at me in the mirror to recognize that throughout my life whenever I've passed by needs—as the priest and the Levite did—instead of coming and seeing and taking pity and helping, it's generally because I've been busy or broke or at odds somehow in my inner world. And I know I'm not alone. As I say, the tendency to place another's needs ahead of our own has never been a natural bent. This remains the case today, which is why across this country and around the globe, food-bank shelves remain empty, schoolchildren remain tutorless, and neighborhoods decimated by natural disasters aren't ever efficiently rebuilt. We don't help because we already feel helpless, as we manage our one and only insular life. We live life so chronically stressed out that those with needs all around us are simply out of luck.

We even have scientific research that bears this out, the idea that harried people generally aren't helpers, that they're too distracted to do any good. In the early 1970s, social psychologists Daniel Batson and John Darley recruited nearly seventy students from the Princeton Theological Seminary and told invitees they would be participating in a study on religious education and vocations. This study is now considered a classic look at helpfulness and its Achilles' heel, hurriedness. After participants completed a straightforward religious questionnaire, they were asked to head to an adjacent building, one by one, where they each would be delivering a brief talk, either on the types of jobs seminary graduates would be good at or on the parable of the good Samaritan.

What participants didn't know was that en route to the adjacent building, they would encounter a man in distress—a plant, courtesy of the research organizers. The man would be found lying in a doorway and doubled over in apparent pain. His eyes would be closed, he would be moaning, and, as if on cue, he would cough exactly twice as each student approached. The students would surely be caught off guard. Had the man been hurt? Was he drunk? Either way, their knee-jerk reactions to the situation would help answer the question being studied: *Who would stop to help?*

The experimenters' hypothesis was that the more hurried the student was, the less likely he or she would be to help. Therefore, they manipulated the study by giving each participant one of three sets of instructions: students were told that (1) they were late and should hurry to the adjacent building; (2) the assistant at the adjacent building was ready for them, so they should head right over; or (3) it would be a few minutes before things would begin at the adjacent building, but that they might as well make their way to the site.

Participants, then, were unwittingly divided into three categories: high hurry, medium hurry, and low hurry. In addition, as you'll recall, half were told to prepare to deliver a talk on job prospects, while the other half expected to give a talk on the parable of the good Samaritan. In this way, researchers could assess both circumstances—the urgency factor and motivation (what was currently on their minds).

It came as no surprise, really, when only 10 percent of high-hurry students offered any sort of help to the man in need. (The harried aren't helpful, remember?) Furthermore, only half of those who were headed to the adjacent building *to deliver a talk on the Good Samaritan* offered to be a Good Samaritan—in any form—to the suffering man that day. I found this note from the researchers interesting: "Some [participants in this category] literally stepped over the victim on their way to the next building!"

A conclusion, among several, was this: "Ethics become a luxury as the speed of our daily lives increases."[5] In other words, we don't have time to be do-gooders, when doing good will take too much of our time.

We can do better than this, can't we? We can meet needs in a needy world. Can't we? Please, please tell me we can. I want to believe that we can. And yet even as my desire skyrockets for believing this way, I come across articles such as this:

> Stress levels for Americans have taken a decidedly downward turn across the USA—except for young adults, whose stress is higher than the national norm, says a survey to be released Thursday.
>
> Those ages 18-33—the Millennial generation—are plenty stressed, and it's not letting up: 39% say their stress has increased in the past year; 52% say stress has kept them awake at night in the past

month. And more than any other age group, they
report being told by a health care provider that they
have either depression or an anxiety disorder.[6]

The study goes on to say one in five adults in this country
between the ages of eighteen and thirty-three is clinically stressed
out, "depressed" even, and in need of medication ... fast.

We've passed "hurry" on to our kids. Our stress is their stress now.

Something in me says it doesn't have to be this way, that we
can reclaim our lives—and theirs—for peace. We can change. We
can, and we should. What's the alternative, really? Spiraling out of
control, passing on the death spiral to our kids, and all of us leaving
this planet totally exhausted someday? What kind of life is that?

"If we stay where we are," Anne Lamott wrote, "where we're
stuck, where we're comfortable and safe, we die there. We become
like mushrooms, living in the dark, with poop up to our chins. If
you want to know only what you already know, you're dying. You're
saying: Leave me alone; I don't mind this little rathole. It's warm and
dry. Really, it's fine."[7] But the little "rathole" isn't fine. Is it? Are we
really okay with turmoil and pain? Are we really happy here, slath-
ered in poop?

I dare say the answer is no.

KEEPING OUR APPOINTMENTS WITH GOD

I was talking with a friend recently about the benefits of rest, which
is what I tend to be talking to everyone about these days. She was

lamenting the rigors of raising young kids, explaining how she couldn't rest: too much to do, too little time to do it, and on and on it went. I think she wanted a pass from me, a little permission, maybe some grace. What she got instead was a sermon. And a really good sermon, at that. Here it is, free of charge.

As she was talking/whining, the thought occurred to me that Adam and Eve ultimately missed out on an entire lifetime of rest because they missed a single, critical appointment with God.

As the book of Genesis tells it, the only thing the first human beings had on their to-do list was a restful, easygoing meeting with God. And yet it's the one thing they didn't get done. From the very beginning, the environment God had put them in was peaceful, restful, and *good*. "The LORD God made all kinds of trees grow out of the ground," Genesis 2:9 says, "trees that were pleasing to the eye and good for food" (NIV). This was a place of abundance. This was a place of calm. And yet the day came when they did what God asked them not to do, and the tranquil enoughness all went away. They ate from the tree God said not to eat from, and sin unceremoniously entered the world.

At the end of Genesis 2, it says that Adam and Eve were so at peace in their garden that they felt exactly zero shame. "No shame" is the perfect description of two souls beautifully at rest. But then comes chapter 3—perhaps the greatest read-it-and-weep story of all time. The setup is a familiar one: Satan, disguised as a serpent, speaks to Eve, challenging the instructions God had given to her. Eve, now persuaded to eat from the tree God specifically said not to touch, takes the fruit and consumes it, and then passes it to Adam, who follows suit. Immediately, they are changed. Their entire world has changed.

God then takes a walk through the garden and calls to Adam, "Where are you?" To which Adam says, "I heard you in the garden, and I was afraid because I was naked; so I hid" (vv. 9–10 NIV).

From there, the truth tumbles out—as the truth always does—that Adam and Eve had defied God's orders and thus separated themselves from the beautiful intimacy with him they'd known. God responded to this situation by detailing a laundry list of sufferings that humankind would now face, and then he expelled his firstborn creation to a far less idyllic way of life.

It was a contrast that was hard to miss. Where there had been quiet strolls, togetherness, evening breezes, and a pervading sense of peace, there were now deception, blaming, enmity, and strife—not just for now, but for always. In the flash of an eye, Adam and Eve were robbed of many things—all their own doing, of course—but the greatest loss, I have to believe, was the permanent loss of rest. There is the sense as you read of the effects of their sin that they'd have to scratch out a living the hard way from now on, that a deep-seated rest would no longer be theirs. In refusing to be found by God, they compromised a lifetime of rest.

We'd shake our heads in astonishment over the stupidity of such neglect, except that we're just as guilty as they are. On a thousand days in a thousand ways, you and I also hide from God. But perhaps unlike Adam and Eve that day, it's not that we don't want to be found by our heavenly Father; it's that we're not sure we remember how. "Human society has moved far east of Eden," wrote Brian Zahnd, "but we still retain in memory the promise of paradise … and how we long to get back to the garden! But is it possible? We know a lot, we have amassed information, we possess sophisticated technology, but we don't know how to find our way back to Eden. We've wandered so far east."[8]

If I had to pinpoint why I'm writing this book, it is to convey one message: *You haven't wandered so far east of Eden that God's rest is not near to you.* It was a single, critical missed appointment with God that thrust everything in the wrong direction, and it is a single, critical kept appointment with him that will begin to set everything right. Tiny disciplines tend to win great wars. When we quit hiding—even for a moment—God says, "I'm here. Let me give you rest. And then from that place of restedness, I'll help you to be light in a very dark world."

LET'S QUIT COMMITTING SPIRITUAL SUICIDE

I'm back in the habit each Sunday morning of closing New Life's worship services with a passionate plea for the entire congregation to go home and take a nap, and based on the Monday morning tweets I've been getting, the weekly exhortation seems to be working. I hear about record-breaking snoozes, drool-soaked pillows, entire halves of televised football games missed—the whole works. And I can't help but smile. This is good news to me. Our people are learning to push Pause on all that needs to happen in their world and simply surrender to rest.

"To keep Sabbath means to stop," Keri Kent said. "Stop working, stop telling people what to do, stop running your household. See if you can model restfulness well enough that your calm pervades your home and even your family."[9] I'm watching this unfold in and around our church, and I assure you, it's a welcomed change. What I'm really telling them, up there from the platform, is this: "Just for today, quit being the master of your universe, and yield to God instead. Be available to him." What I'm saying, in a soulish sense, is, "Be willing to be found."

Last week, one of the guys at New Life took his family out to lunch after church and then went home and took what he described as "a monster nap." (Good for him!) Hours later he woke and told his wife he was headed to the gas station a couple of miles away, to fill up their two cars for the week ahead. He returned after refueling the first car, and when his wife happened upon him, he was rifling through a basket of umbrellas the family keeps in a hall closet. When she asked what he was up to, he said, "It's pouring outside, and there's a couple standing in the rain on the interstate—right at our exit. I figured they could have one of these."

I should tell you straight up that this story doesn't have some world-altering ending. The guy drove the family's second car over to the gas station—as planned—and on his way, he was prepared to roll down his window and offer the drenched couple an umbrella and any other help they might need. He was disappointed to discover that the couple was no longer there, but the outcome is not what I homed in on; his *availability* is. This New Lifer was findable; he was findable to his God.

I want to be findable to God too. I want to live life like that every day: accessible, available, and *all-the-way alive*.

To live all-the-way alive is, in the words of Eugene Peterson, to explore the "unforced rhythms of grace" (Matt. 11:29). What does exploring those unforced rhythms look like? It looks like bringing life to those around us, not out of obligation, but out of overflow.

It looks like people who simply can't help but to be helpful to those who really need help.

It looks like at last having eyes to see.

We see the neighbor whose car won't start; the clerk with distant eyes; the mom of young kids juggling both a stroller and a shopping cart; the couple standing on the corner in a downpour, now soaking wet. Yes, we still see our to-do list: we're trying to mow the lawn or buy the groceries or get gas and get back home. But somehow our priorities have shifted; the people have trumped the task. Well-rested "light in a very dark world," if you'll recall … this is how we come alive.

It's a bold vision, I realize; if you survey our relational landscape today, you'll see we have a long, long way to go. We're disconnected from one another, even in this age of connectivity, electronic-style. But is this a surprise to anyone? You and I both know in our gut that a one-on-one interaction beats the virtual kind every time, and yet still we while away our time with our smartphones in hand, tweeting and posting and commenting and emailing, failing at every turn to truly "connect." We're as glazed over and distracted as those young conference goers in our church's parking lot I told you about at the beginning of this book, noses glued to technology's latest thing. We're alive, but you'd hardly know it. We're dying before we're dead.

A recent report shows that more Americans now die of suicide than in car accidents and that gun suicides are almost twice as common as gun homicides.[10] It's a sobering statistic, this idea that so many are taking their own lives. Here's what the current studies fail to report: the multiplied numbers of those who are committing suicide of the spiritual sort. We've allowed ourselves to die inside; we have no life to offer, to a world flatlining before our eyes.

We've got to pull together. We've got to engage, real time. We've got to help the helpless. We've got to come alive.

We've got to embrace rhythmic living so that, as Wayne Muller encouraged, "when we go forth to heal the wounds of our world, whatever we build, create, craft, or serve will have the wisdom of rest in it."[11] What a compelling concept! It's the difference between eating fast food and sitting down to a meal that has been prepared with patience and love. A vast difference, wouldn't you say? I dare say the same is true when we parent from a place of peace or lead a meeting from a place of peace or have a difficult conversation with our spouse from a place of peace, or interact with a retail clerk from a place of peace, or do any of a thousand other daily things we're always finding ourselves doing—all from a place of peace. *Everything goes better when that thing is done from a place of peace.* Not only are we living the life that is truly life, but we're also spreading that "truly life" life around. This is peer pressure in its finest form, really. This is who you and I both want to be. When we show up and when we share peace, we become the people we were intended to be.

When Pam and I first arrived in Colorado—this would have been the first or second week of August 2007—it was for a three-week "audition" before the staff and congregation of New Life Church. For three consecutive Sundays, I was asked to preach my life messages—the sermons that best demonstrate my view of God, my view of the world, and my understanding of what it means to be a Christ follower in this day and age. It was awful. I mean, it was great in that if I did well, I'd be voted in as the new senior pastor. But it was awful to feel like a contestant on a reality show, someone desperate for the applause of the crowd.

The Saturday before my first Sunday talk, I was a nervous wreck. I wasn't nervous about preaching; I was nervous about the result of my preaching. Old demons came back to haunt me: What if they didn't like me? What if they didn't accept me? What if the best I could do was ultimately declared not enough?

Pam and I drove around all day Saturday, checking out the city that we hoped would be our new home. I distinctly remember that we were on the far north side of town, when Pam all but insisted we drive half an hour south to eat lunch at a particular Mexican food restaurant. There are scores of Mexican food options up north, which is why her demand was so odd to me. That, and Pam is almost never demanding. This was very out of character in my view.

To add to the oddness, I kept catching her checking her watch, there in the passenger seat. She seemed jittery, as though we were late for something. Of course we weren't; the only plan we had was to burn up hours until I stepped onto the platform Sunday morning to preach. Maybe she was just nervous about the audition. Given my own anxious state, that certainly would make sense.

I finally conceded to Pam's wishes and navigated to the requested restaurant a half-hour's drive away, only to be told by her once we were seated that we couldn't order food yet. I looked at my wife, who was growing stranger to me by the moment. "But I'm hungry!" I said, to which she said, "I'd like to wait for a few minutes. Here. Have a few more chips."

We were on our third basket of tortilla chips when the door to the restaurant flew open and four of my closest friends from Texas casually strolled in. Suddenly everything became clear. My best buddies had flown all the way to Colorado, to be with me during my first weekend at what would be my new church.

I jumped up and grabbed Morgan first and then bear-hugged Peter, Shawn, and Marcus, each in turn. And then I exhaled every last concern that had been needlessly overtaking my heart. These were busy men—business owners and high-flying executives, each of them a husband, a dad—and yet they'd taken two days out of their schedules to come to me in one of my deepest points of need. I might as well have been lying on the side of the road, just like in the parable, bloodied and beaten to a pulp—emotionally, my need was that great. And yet the mere presence of four devoted friends bound my wounds, turning fear to faith in a flash. They were doing their thing from a place of peace, and they spread peace to me as a result.

We sat out on the back deck that night at the house where my family was staying and told the same old stories we've recounted a hundred times and enjoyed in equal measure one another's company and a cool August breeze. They sat with me until nine or ten that night and then headed for their hotel as I made my way to bed.

The following morning, I would turn around in my seat there in the front row of New Life's auditorium and see four familiar faces smiling back. I didn't know a soul in the vast congregation, but I did know these four men, men whose faces shone like pure gold.

I rose from my seat when it was my time to preach, taking in stride the eight steps to the stage. I delivered my talk in peace, amazed by my good turn of heart. My friends' presence was steadiness in uncertainty's storm, needed silence for my noisy heart.[12] Richard Rohr says, "Silence is the necessary space around things that allows them to develop and flourish without my pushing." My four peacemakers had brought me to silence in all her glory. Silence, stillness, okayness—this is exactly what I craved.

LIVING FULLY ALIVE

All these years later I reflect on that occasion, thinking, *I wonder, what radical things would I do, if I were living fully alive?*

Think about it. If you and I had margin, if we weren't chronically stressed out, if we weren't forever dashing from here to there to there … I wonder what we'd do differently, what we'd attempt, who we'd become.

Three pieces of advice, if you're interested in answering that question for yourself. First, *unplug*. Decide now that the rhythmic life is worth living, that *peaceful* describes the person you want to become. Next, *be filled*. Know what brings you alive and pursue it. Be intentional during unplugged times. And third, *give your best away*. Share your sense of peace with a world in chaos, letting the abundance of your life overflow.

This is how we quit dying inside. It's how we come alive.

THE FULLY ALIVE *UNPLUG*

A mom of a newborn mentioned yesterday that her baby has been awake the last two nights and has been sleeping the last two days and joked that maybe her little one is "part owl." She said she and her husband never knew just how beautifully active the night sky was; they'd spent all those years sleeping through it!

It's a common thing, evidently, babies getting daytime and nighttime mixed up. I know this mom. In fact, it was exactly one year ago next Tuesday that I told this now-forty-seven-year-old woman and her husband not to give up on having a child. They had tried everything infertile couples try, to no avail, but God spoke to my heart one day that this couple should not give up. And so I told them to persevere.

They did persevere, and now, twelve months later, a tiny daughter lives in their home.

It has been a long road for them, a wearying road for them, which is why I was so delighted to see she was taking this day/night mix-up in stride.

I'm sure there are a thousand baby psychologists out there with strong opinions on every newborn dilemma imaginable, including how to get your child to sleep when it's time to sleep, but here is what I thought as I listened to that loving mom: *You are getting it so right. The books and blogs and theories and rants will still be there a few weeks from now. Today, keep choosing rest. Your baby will thank you for it someday.*

The same is true for us all. Now is the time for rest. For getting our bearings. For talking with God. For choosing to unplug. The dilemmas that need solving will still be there when tomorrow dawns. For today, let's agree to relinquish them, to drop our shoulders, and to simply pick peace.

THE FULLY ALIVE *GET FILLED*

Last month, I went to a pastors' meeting hosted by the senior pastor of another local church. Ironically the meeting was about effective sabbaticals—how to "enforce" them, what they should look like, how long they should be. He had a written policy he gives to his staff—this guy meant business about rest!

His basic premise was this: when we—and by "we," I mean well-meaning, Christ-following people who are trying to live rhythmic lives—finally agree to take some time off (a stay-cation, a vacation, an official sabbatical, whatever), we pretty much stink at being intentional with that time. And so my colleague created a policy—a policy to enforce core principles of rest.

I balked at the idea of systemizing rest, until he handed out copies of the rules, of which there were three: retreat, refresh your soul, and renew your focus. That's it—the three tenets of effective rest. He went on to explain to those of us gathered there that rest requires a plan or else it becomes a superficial vacation, a rigorous academic leave, or an unhelpful escape. This, of course, begged the question from several of us: "What does your plan usually involve?"

He was preparing for an upcoming sabbatical, as it turned out, and he was more than happy to reveal to us his plan. "Well, I'm going to a bluegrass music festival," he said. "I'm going to take my guitar and write some songs and watch the sun go down and drink beer." This elicited some chuckles from the crowd. In his button-down oxford, argyle sweater, and old-school pleated pants, this pastor looked more like an accountant than an artist.

"You guys think I'm joking!" he said, laughing. "But I tell you what, I'm not." And then he said this, which stuck with me for weeks following the session: "You've got to know what makes you come alive."

He said that a few days in an environment like that—being outdoors, meeting new people, listening to great music, ditching "work clothes" in favor of shorts—would utterly renovate his heart. He'd be able to reflect and write and breathe in ways he's not able to while at home.

After the collective group had a few more good-natured laughs at his expense, he told us how he'd hatched the grand idea. "I was journaling one day about what makes my heart race in a good way, what makes me feel most alive, and what I landed on was all this—music, warmth, sunshine, and so forth—and so I built my sabbatical around those things."

What began as a lighthearted discussion ended on a gut-level note. This guy had hit on something big. We *all* should make such lists.

What does make me come alive? I wondered. And so began my own introspection—a journal, a pen, and me.

For starters, my list included palm trees, salty air, and an ocean within walking distance. Warmth. The sound of seagulls squawking nearby. When Pam and I were first married and were living in northwest Louisiana—miles and miles from any semblance of a beach—we had one of those sound machines that played ocean waves. I'd listen to that thing every night and be transported in my mind. I know I live in paradise, here in the Rocky Mountain region, but the ocean is what really makes me come alive.

Of course my list also included international travel. Spending time immersed in a different culture, surrounded by different sights, sounds, and sensations than what I experience in my daily life is a sure way to bring me life.

And then there was sitting outside during a rainstorm, preferably on a covered porch. Twenty minutes later, I'm a man reborn.

And finally, a little solitude, being alone in the presence of God.

We don't think about this question enough, but we ought to: *What makes us come alive?* What makes our pulses race, our hearts soar, and our most challenging circumstances for the moment fade to gray?

I think about the Good Samaritan and wonder what had fueled his act of kindness toward that man on the side of the road. Had he spent the previous day watching a rainstorm? Enjoying a good novel? Taking his kids to the beach?

Mission requires margin. One thing we can be sure of is that somehow, he'd been filled up.

THE FULLY ALIVE *GIVE THEIR BEST AWAY*

Several months ago, Abram and I were having breakfast together at a local café and spotted a couple from New Life sitting a dozen or so booths away. They were deep in conversation, and so we didn't approach; as far as I know, we weren't noticed by either of them as the hostess led us to our table across the room. After we placed our order, I asked our server if she was also covering that table, the one where the New Lifers still sat. "I'd like you to add their bill to ours without their knowing," I said. She smiled conspiratorially and said, "No problem. Consider it done."

I had met with this particular couple just a few months prior, when they requested a conversation about their current financial mess. They went on to enroll in money-management classes New Life offers, and I had received an email from the husband saying they were getting back on track. But still, the twenty-dollar tab would have to be accounted for, and when you're dead broke, every dollar hurts.

After the server headed back to the kitchen, Abram asked what was going on. I didn't want to betray the couple's confidence—even to my son—and so I simply explained that when God gives us an extra twenty bucks (or an extra twenty minutes, or an extra twenty *anything*), there is nothing better to do with it than to quickly give it away. Mission requires margin ... there it is yet again. It's a lesson I'm still learning, and one I hope to pass along to my kids.

When you and I seize upon that lifestyle of rest, that lifestyle of healthy rhythms, that lifestyle of bringing life and not death with us, wherever we go, not only do we live fulfilled, but we also help point others toward the fulfillment we so desperately sought. Yes, it's true that we can't give what we don't have, but equally true is that we can give what we do. When our cups are full—or at least are not bone dry—we have a reservoir from which to draw.

Jan Johnson tucks this idea into the context of our weekly ritual of going to church. "Simplicity leads to greater abundance in life," she wrote. "Because disciplines of simplicity [read: margin, "find-ability," peacefulness, rest] create more space to experience fellowship with God, we no longer drag our impoverished selves to church every week to get 'fixed' spiritually. For example, if we decide not to spend time on the Internet and take a walk instead, we have a chance to ask ourselves what we're most grateful for today."[13]

"With such a God-nurtured lifestyle," she continues, "we don't need a maximum-style weekend experience to get us through the week. We begin trusting God's very own self in daily life so that when we fellowship with others at church, we have more to give."

And then this, my favorite line of the entire passage: "The abiding life overflows."[14]

You and I are overflowing with *something*; I'll guarantee you that. Either we're overflowing with peace and rest, or we're leaving turmoil and chaos in our wake. If I get to pick, I pick the former, not the latter. I want to bring good stuff with me as I come, and leave good stuff behind me long after I go.

What I've wished for I'm now experiencing, a life so filled with abundance that it overflows like that Sabbath-night kiddush cup. I am reminded of the way Eugene Peterson reimagined Psalm 23:5, and I take heart. "You revive my drooping head," verse 5 reads. "My cup brims with blessing."

I whisper it to God as a prayer of thanksgiving. "You have revived my drooping head, Lord. And now my cup—it overflows."

BREAKING BUSY

Challenge #1: Dream a Little

Spend a few minutes thinking about what you would do on others' behalf, if only you had a little more margin in your life. Without editing for feasibility, jot down on a piece of paper the ideas that come to mind. Would you host a dinner party for the new neighbors who just moved in three doors down? Would you sign up to serve at the soup kitchen downtown? Would you agree to help out in children's ministry? Would you take time out of your precious weekend to visit someone who is homebound or imprisoned or hospitalized? Would you help tutor underprivileged kids? Would you show up at the weekly prayer meeting? Would you invite the guy who is homeless to come have lunch with you at a restaurant for once?

Let your thoughts take you wherever they want to go. Your only job here is to record them.

Challenge #2: Live Out That Dream

Now, start living your dream. Maybe not the full list all at once, but at least some part of the list. If a little extra margin in your life would mean hosting a dinner party for your new neighbors, then step one here is simply walking down the street, introducing yourself, and offering to help carry in moving boxes. Have a conversation—let that be step number one in your new rhythmic way of life. The other steps will come, once you agree to make that first move.

Consider coming back to your dream list throughout the year, and see if God doesn't afford you custom-fitted opportunities to make every last one of those dreams come true.

NOTES

Introduction—This Book Won't Change Your Life

1. Anne Lamott, *Help, Thanks, Wow: The Three Essential Prayers* (New York: Riverhead, 2012), 52, 53.

Part One—Epigraph

Leonard Sweet spoke these words in a talk attended by Brady Boyd. For a brilliant discussion on this theme of being too busy for God, check out Sweet's 2014 book, *The Well-Played Life* (Carol Stream, IL: Tyndale, 2014).

Chapter 1—Dead Husband Walking

1. Richard A. Swenson, MD, *Margin: Restoring Emotional, Physical, Financial, and Time Reserves to Overloaded Lives* (Colorado Springs, CO: NavPress, 1992), 29.
2. Wayne Muller, *Sabbath: Finding Rest, Renewal, and Delight in Our Busy Lives* (New York: Bantam, 1999), 20.

Chapter 2—Restless Bodies, Restless Minds

1. Daniel Goleman, *Social Intelligence: The New Science of Human Relationships* (New York: Bantam, 2006), 267.
2. Dr. Archibald D. Hart, *Adrenaline and Stress: The Exciting New Breakthrough That Helps You Overcome Stress Damage* (Nashville: Thomas Nelson, 1995), 40.
3. 2 Corinthians 10:5 NIV.
4. Matthew 22:37 NIV.
5. Philippians 2:5 NIV.
6. See Philippians 4:8 NIV.
7. Colossians 3:2 NIV.
8. Psalm 139:17 NIV.

9. Wayne Muller, *Sabbath: Finding Rest, Renewal, and Delight in Our Busy Lives* (New York: Bantam, 1999), 18.

Chapter 3—Distraction Versus Devotion

1. Matthew Sleeth, MD, *24/6: A Prescription for a Healthier, Happier Life* (Carol Stream, IL: Tyndale, 2012), 107.

2. Bob Sullivan, "How the Smartphone Killed the Three-Day Weekend," CNBC Technology, www.cnbc.com/id/100765600.

3. Christine Sine, MD, *Sacred Rhythms: Finding a Peaceful Pace in a Hectic World* (Grand Rapids, MI: Baker, 2003), 26.

4. Wayne Muller, *Sabbath: Finding Rest, Renewal, and Delight in Our Busy Lives* (New York: Bantam, 1999), 19.

Chapter 4—Being Who We Are

1. Lauren Sherman, "Twenty Most Affluent U.S. Neighborhoods," *Forbes*, December 9, 2008, www.forbes.com/2008/12/08/america-affluent-neighborhoods-forbeslife -cx_ls_1209realestate.html.

2. "Southlake, Texas," City-Data.com, www.city-data.com/city/Southlake-Texas. html.

3. Tim Kreider, "The 'Busy' Trap," The Opinion Pages, *New York Times*, June 30, 2012, http://opinionator.blogs.nytimes.com/2012/06/30/the-busy-trap/?_php=true &_type=blogs&_r=0.

4. "Evelyn Underhill Quotes," Goodreads.com, www.goodreads.com/author/quotes /112836.Evelyn_Underhill.

5. "N.Y. Jet Crash Called 'Miracle on the Hudson,'" NBCNews.com, January 15, 2009, www.nbcnews.com/id/28678669/ns/us_news-life/t/ny-jet-crash-called -miracle-hudson.

6. "Ric Elias: 3 Things I Learned While My Plane Crashed," TED Talks, www.ted. com/talks/ric_elias.html.

7. Mark Buchanan, *The Rest of God: Restoring Your Soul by Restoring Sabbath* (Nashville: Thomas Nelson, 2006), 93.

8. Anne Lamott, *Help, Thanks, Wow: The Three Essential Prayers* (New York: Riverhead, 2012), 85.

Chapter 5—Shabbat Shalom

1. "What Is the Meaning of 'Shabbat Shalom,'" Jews and Joes, jewsandjoes.com/what-is-the-meaning-of-shabbat-shalom.html.

2. Mark Buchanan, *The Rest of God: Restoring Your Soul by Restoring Sabbath* (Nashville: Thomas Nelson, 2006), 59.

3. "Night Prayer," *A New Zealand Prayer Book*, http://anglicanprayerbook.org.nz/167.html, 184.

4. Buchanan, *The Rest of God*, 90.

5. Brian Zahnd, *Beauty Will Save the World: Rediscovering the Allure and Mystery of Christianity* (Lake Mary, FL: Charisma House, 2012), 141. If you haven't yet read *Beauty*, stop reading this book and pick up that one. Game changer, for sure.

6. Tim Kreider, "The 'Busy' Trap," The Opinion Pages, *New York Times*, June 30, 2012, http://opinionator.blogs.nytimes.com/2012/06/30/the-busy-trap/?_php=true&_type=blogs&_r=0.

7. Katrina Kenison, *Mitten Strings for God: Reflections for Mothers in a Hurry* (New York: Warner, 2002), 15.

8. MaryAnn McKibben Dana, *Sabbath in the Suburbs: A Family's Experiment with Holy Time* (St. Louis, MO: Chalice, 2012), 38.

Chapter 6—The Jesus Pace

1. See Luke 9:23.

2. See Matthew 14:12–13.

3. See Luke 6:12–13.

4. See Luke 5:16.

5. See Matthew 26:36–46.

6. See Mark 6:30–32.

7. Wayne Muller, *Sabbath: Finding Rest, Renewal, and Delight in Our Busy Lives* (New York: Bantam, 1999), 25.

8. Senator Joseph Lieberman, *The Gift of Rest: Rediscovering the Beauty of the Sabbath* (New York: Howard Books, 2011), 33.

9. D. A. Carson, ed., *From Sabbath to Lord's Day: A Biblical, Historical, and Theological Investigation* (Eugene, OR: Wipf and Stock, 1999), 34–35.

10. "Pedro Arrupe Quotes," Goodreads.com, www.goodreads.com/author/quotes /316647.Pedro_Arrupe.

11. If this were a glowing account, I'd have opted for using his real name.

Chapter 7—Choosing My Vine

1. John M. Grohol, "FOMO Addiction: The Fear of Missing Out," PsychCentral.com, http://psychcentral.com/blog/archives/2011/04/14/fomo -addiction-the-fear-of-missing-out/.

2. Constance Rhodes, *The Art of Being: Reflections on the Beauty and the Risk of Embracing Who We Are* (Colorado Springs, CO: Shaw, 2004), 118–19.

3. Brian Zahnd, *Beauty Will Save the World: Rediscovering the Allure and Mystery of Christianity* (Lake Mary, FL: Charisma House, 2012), 22–23.

4. Jan Johnson, *Abundant Simplicity: Discovering the Unhurried Rhythms of Grace* (Downers Grove, IL: InterVarsity, 2011), 107.

5. Jonathan Martin, *Prototype: What Happens When You Discover You're More Like Jesus Than You Think?* (Carol Stream, IL: Tyndale, 2013), 48.

6. Catherine de Hueck Doherty, *Poustinia: Encountering God in Silence, Solitude and Prayer* (Combermere, Ontario: Madonna House Publishers, 2012), 5–6.

7. "Martin Smith Interview: The Delirious? Years (Part 1 of 2)," www.youtube.com /watch?v=df25nXpiLEo.

8. See Martin, *Prototype*, 49.

Chapter 8—What to Do on a Do-Nothing Day

1. Dan Allender, *Sabbath: The Ancient Practices Series* (Nashville: Thomas Nelson, 2009), 38.

2. Keri Wyatt Kent, *Rest: Living in Sabbath Simplicity* (Grand Rapids, MI: Zondervan, 2009), 23–24; italics mine.

3. Allender, *Sabbath*, 86.

4. Rachel Held Evans, *A Year of Biblical Womanhood: How a Liberated Woman Found Herself Sitting on Her Roof, Covering Her Head, and Calling Her Husband "Master"* (Nashville: Thomas Nelson, 2012), 273–74, 275.

5. Katherine Ellison, "Full Bio," www.katherineellison.com.

6. Katherine Ellison, *Buzz: A Year of Paying Attention* (New York: Hyperion, 2010), 83.

7. Ellison, *Buzz*, 5.

8. Ellison, *Buzz*, 7.

9. Ellison, *Buzz*, 101.

10. Ellison, *Buzz*, 205.

11. Ellison, *Buzz*, 76.

12. Richard A. Swenson, MD, *Margin: Restoring Emotional, Physical, Financial, and Time Reserves to Overloaded Lives* (Colorado Springs, CO: NavPress, 1992), 77.

Chapter 9—Three Things I Wish I'd Known

1. John Eldredge, *Waking the Dead: The Glory of a Heart Fully Alive* (Nashville: Thomas Nelson, 2003), 218.

2. Daniel Goleman, *Social Intelligence: The New Science of Human Relationships* (New York: Bantam, 2006), 68.

3. Dallas Willard, *The Spirit of the Disciplines: Understanding How God Changes Lives* (New York: HarperCollins, 1988), 56.

4. Brother Lawrence, *The Practice of the Presence of God* (Nashville: Thomas Nelson, 1999), 20–21.

5. D. Martyn Lloyd-Jones, *Studies in the Sermon on the Mount* (Grand Rapids, MI: Eerdmans, 1976), 294–5.

Chapter 10—Come Alive

1. See Luke 10 for the full biblical account.

2. Brooke Hromadka, "Good Samaritan (Kids)—Springs Rescue Mission," www .youtube.com/watch?v=9wSX7NTJFLg; produced by Springs Rescue Mission, Colorado Springs.

3. Maayana Miskin, "Plans to Use Christmas, New Year to Bring the Messiah," Arutz Sheva 7, December 23, 2010, www.israelnationalnews.com/News/News.aspx /141300.

4. Senator Joseph Lieberman, *The Gift of Rest: Rediscovering the Beauty of the Sabbath* (New York: Howard Books, 2011), 223.

5. John Darley and Daniel Batson, "From Jerusalem to Jericho: A Study of Situational and Dispositional Variables in Helping Behavior," http://faculty. babson.edu/krollag/org_site/soc_psych/darley_samarit.html.

6. Sharon Jayson, "Who's Feeling Stressed? Young Adults, New Survey Shows," *USA Today*, February 7, 2013, www.usatoday.com/story/news/nation/2013/02/06/stress -psychology-millennials-depression/1878295/.

7. Anne Lamott, *Help, Thanks, Wow: The Three Essential Prayers* (New York: Riverhead, 2012), 86.

8. Brian Zahnd, *Beauty Will Save the World: Rediscovering the Allure and Mystery of Christianity* (Lake Mary, FL: Charisma House, 2012), 102.

9. Keri Wyatt Kent, *Rest: Living in Sabbath Simplicity* (Grand Rapids, MI: Zondervan, 2009), 101.

10. Ross Douthat, "All the Lonely People," The Opinion Pages, *New York Times*, May 19, 2013, www.nytimes.com/2013/05/19/opinion/sunday/douthat-loneliness -and-suicide.html.

11. Wayne Muller, *Sabbath: Finding Rest, Renewal, and Delight in Our Busy Lives* (New York: Bantam, 2006), 10.

12. I first learned this phrase—"noisy heart"—in Richard J. Foster's *Sanctuary of the Soul* (Downers Grove, IL: InterVarsity, 2011).

13. Jan Johnson, *Abundant Simplicity: Discovering the Unhurried Rhythms of Grace* (Downers Grove, IL: InterVarsity, 2011), 19–20.

14. Johnson, *Abundant Simplicity*, 20.